Praise for *The McKinsey Engagement*

*"A useful methodology that student consulting teams (and
many other types of teams as well) can immediately
implement and realize significant benefits."*
—James W. Dean, Jr.,
Dean, Kenan-Flagler Business School,
University of North Carolina at Chapel Hill

*"Essential for any business to move beyond
opinion and address reality."*
—Dr. Charles Lucier,
Senior Vice-President Emeritus,
Booz Allen Hamilton

"The McKinsey Engagement *is a guide for team problem
solving that will improve results for internal and external
consultants in businesses across the globe. Veterans will
identify best practices from their experience, while learning
insights to improve efficiency and effectiveness.
Newcomers will find a blueprint for success, complete
with practical tools and techniques."*
—Retired Partner,
Ernst & Young LLP

THE
McKINSEY
ENGAGEMENT

**A POWERFUL TOOLKIT FOR
MORE EFFICIENT & EFFECTIVE
TEAM PROBLEM SOLVING**

THE
McKINSEY
ENGAGEMENT

PAUL N. FRIGA, Ph.D.

New York   Chicago   San Francisco   Lisbon   London   Madrid   Mexico City
Milan   New Delhi   San Juan   Seoul   Singapore   Sydney   Toronto

The *McGraw·Hill* Companies

3 4 5 6 7 8 9 0 QFR/QFR 0 1 0

ISBN 978-0-07-149741-1
MHID   0-07-149741-2

This book is printed on acid-free paper.

McGraw-Hill books are available at special quantity discounts to use as premiums and sales promotions, or for use in corporate training programs. To contact a representative please visit the Contact Us pages at www.mhprofessional.com.

Library of Congress Cataloging-in-Publication Data

Friga, Paul N.
    The McKinsey engagement : a powerful toolkit for more efficient and effective
    team problem solving / by Paul N. Friga.
        p. cm.
    Includes bibliographical references and index.
    ISBN 0-07-149741-2 (alk. paper)
1. Group problem solving—Handbooks, manuals, etc.   I. Title.
    HD30.29.F75 2009
    658.4'022—dc22

                                   2008023117

CONTENTS

ACKNOWLEDGMENTS

There are so many amazing people who have contributed to making this book possible. I hesitate to try to document them for fear of omission, but I will give it the old college try.

MY FAMILY

My Wife, Meredith—the love of my life who inspires me
  every day
My Son, Nicholas—who teaches me just how precious life is
My Dad—who still lives with me today
My Mom—who keeps me focused on the important things
My Brother—who always offers a fresh intellectual perspective
My Sister—who is a constant source of positive energy
My Uncle Rich—who is always ready for a great conversation
My Uncle Joe—who thinks he has a good sense of humor
The Lord—who makes all things possible

MY SUPERSTAR RESEARCH ASSISTANT

Emi Ruble, without whom this book would not have been written. She worked with me from the beginning on brainstorming, outlining, researching, interviewing, editing, and most of all writing. She essentially wrote the entire case study that plays such a critical role in this book. One day, she will be a famous author and English professor, and I just hope that she remembers me (only the positive memories of course)!

MY KELLEY SCHOOL OF BUSINESS RESEARCH TEAM

Drew Allenspach
Dimitra Bourgis
Chris Cannon
Jatin Karani
Peter Kuo
Steve McGuire
Kendall Miller
Abhi Nadgir
Maddy Vishnu Nampoothiri
Emi Ruble
Jessica Wild

THE MBA CASE STUDY TEAM

Alan Burleson
Chris Cannon

Tim Krzywicki
Shalini Makkar
Bhavin Shah
Rachita Sundar

THE REVIEWERS

Rich Chapas
Joe Harbert
Marilyn Friga
Meredith Friga
Tony Gerth
Bill Gilliland
Michael Meeks
Matt Semadeni

THE KELLEY MANAGEMENT DEPARTMENT ADMINISTRATIVE ASSISTANTS

Lisa Castor
Sarah Fella
Kathy Hakeem
Tammy Tharp

THE INTERVIEWEES (WHO PROVIDED VALUABLE WAR STORIES TO BRING LIFE TO THE BOOK)

Arnaud Beernaert

Clifford Dank

Brigham Frandsen

Tony Gerth

Yannick Grecourt

D. A. Gros

Alain Guy

Fred Humiston

Ben Kennedy

Peter Kuo

Mike Lewis

Victoria Lim

Sisto Merolla

Duncan Orr

Mario Pellizzari

Oliver Personnaz

Dr. Florian Pfeffel

Juan Pulido

Pedro Ramos

Rob Torti

Mike Yang

And the dozens of additional interviewees who chose to remain anonymous.

OTHERS (MENTORS, FRIENDS, ACCOMPLICES, ETC.)

Joe Burton

Mike Duke

Idie Kesner

Anita Knowles

Kaihan Krippendorff

Barbara Minto

Peggy Pickard

Rob Richardson

Mitch Ripley

AnaMaria Rivera

Shari Rogge-Fidler

Paul Sansone

Brian Waterman

And Ethan Rasiel, who is my coauthor, friend, and teacher.

PREFACE

The two-person Green Berets sniper team slithered silently through the weed-infested underbrush, completely unnoticed by the sleeping enemy. Weeks of training in terrain navigation made this special-ops mission feel almost like a routine assignment, but the team knew that this was not a drill. Their state-of-the-art night vision goggles provided them with a clear target approximately 100 yards ahead in the pitch-black night. The team leader whispered instructions to the specialized shooter (who had finished first in the rigorous Special Forces Q Course) and radioed back to the base commanders. Everyone in the operation knew exactly what was coming next ... the terrorist radio operator target would be taken out, and the snipers would proceed to the rendezvous point exactly two hours later. And there was no doubt that the mission would be successful; their confidence was based on months of extreme physical and mental conditioning, scenario-based training, and lessons learned from the thousands of Green Berets who had done this before.

After centuries of warfare, military organizations have developed tremendous expertise in many areas that are relevant to modern-day corporations. Numerous books have been written on leadership lessons (for example, one of the first I read was *Leadership Secrets of Attila the Hun*), organizational structure, and strategies (*The Art of War* by Sun Tzu is required reading at the CEO level and in some strategy Ph.D. programs) derived from these organizations. In fact, much of modern business language is borrowed from the military—mission, vision, hierarchy, strategic communication, centralization, specialization, and so on. There is a reason for this: much can be learned from military tactics that can have a positive impact in the business world. In terms of this book, the military concepts of standard operating procedures, excellence in execution, and cross-training offer valuable insights.

James "Mac" McKinsey, a University of Chicago professor, founded McKinsey in 1926. In the 80+ years since, McKinsey has grown to become one of the most successful strategic consulting firms in the world. It has instilled a very structured approach to consulting and has an almost militaristic discipline in its strong culture. The people of McKinsey realize that success in consulting will come only to those players who can operate in a manner that is consistent with the world-class "special forces" of the top military organizations—that is, those with the most extensive training, organizational focus, and consistency in execution.

This book is dedicated to exploring how McKinsey, along with a select few other top consulting firms and some top MBA programs, excels at the most important element of helping clients achieve phenomenal positive returns during consulting interventions: *team problem solving*. Team problem solving occurs when multiple persons are vested in finding the solution to a major issue.

At McKinsey, team problem solving occurs during engagements or studies. In the military, these are considered missions. Regardless of what you call it, almost all major business decisions are the result of team problem solving; because McKinsey is among the best in the world at problem solving, it is able to charge a premium for its much-sought-after services.

My goal is quite simple; to offer a toolkit that can be used to improve the effectiveness and efficiency of any project that involves team problem solving. This book highlights and implements lessons from the "special forces" techniques that are used at McKinsey and other firms for the benefit of a much wider audience. This is not intended to be a very deep or theoretical read; rather, it is intended to be a field guide for busy professionals, consultants, and students who are facing a team problem-solving situation but don't have much time to get to the main point or recommendation.

Have you ever worked on a *perfect* engagement or field study—one that exactly balances interpersonal interaction and analytical horsepower and produces outstanding deliverables? I haven't. We have all worked on terrific teams and great projects, but there was always something that could have been improved. Wouldn't it be nice to have the confidence of an Army Green Beret in your problem solving approach and to have a consistent, cohesive system that leads to world-class, efficient execution throughout your entire firm, organization, or school? I am convinced that a master guide to team problem-solving projects will be a meaningful contribution in this regard.

This book describes the most important lessons (both good and bad) from past projects and the accumulated wisdom of numerous previous problem solvers—both in business and in the military. My experience over the past 20 years has generated ideas for just such a guide. Over the past six years, I have been documenting my ideas, conducting interviews with experts, and developing the concepts contained in this book. My hope is that this material will help consultants, executives, and students achieve the kind of success in team problem solving witnessed at McKinsey and other top consulting firms. I would also like to make a special comment about confidentiality. Nowhere in this book will you find any proprietary, sensitive, or confidential material from McKinsey or any other firm.

THE BACKGROUND

It may be helpful to take a step back in time. My first experiences in project management came during my days at Pricewaterhouse-Coopers (PwC)— then just Price Waterhouse. My tenure at PwC taught me quite a few lessons, witnessing both some of the best-planned engagements (in audits) and some of the worst-planned engagements (in turnaround consulting) you could imagine. I returned to academia after six years at PwC and earned my MBA from the Kenan-Flagler Business School at the University of North Carolina at Chapel Hill. Upon graduation, a door opened for me at the most sought-after consulting firm in the world (McKinsey is consistently ranked as the top position for MBA graduates in annual surveys and is highly regarded for problem-solving methodologies).

After leaving McKinsey, a return to academia to pursue my long-term goal of becoming a professor brought me back to Chapel Hill. It was during my Ph.D. program (again at UNC) that I worked with Ethan Rasiel (the author of *The McKinsey Way*, which describes the culture and processes at McKinsey) to write *The McKinsey Mind*, a book that presents lessons learned from McKinsey alumni who were working to implement takeaways from their time at the "firm" in different organizations. Both books have done quite well and have sold over 100,000 copies in total, with 10+ international language translations as of the time of this writing.

After completing my Ph.D., I taught strategy and management consulting at Indiana University's Kelley School of Business. I just returned to UNC, only this time as a professor in the Kenan-Flagler School of Business. I have also delivered numerous executive and consultant education programs on strategy, management consulting, and strategic thinking. It was during this time that my research on consulting training at many of the top firms helped me to finalize my framework for project management, which is presented in this book.

In writing this book, I wanted to make an incremental contribution to the ideas previously presented in *The McKinsey Way* and *The McKinsey Mind*. The key difference, and my reason for believing that another book will be helpful, involves this book's level of tactical implementation advice. As a starting point, it uses many of the same concepts presented in the model from *The McKinsey Mind* (that model centers on Analysis, Management, and Presentation, which are common to all team problem-solving projects), although they are organized a bit differently and the implementation advice goes to a deeper level.

Many readers of the first two books in the series (as well as the publisher) inquired about the possibility of such a field guide that would have very specific advice for tactical implementation of the ideas, along with more illustrations and tools for using the concepts on team problem-solving projects. That became the focus of my energy. Could I create a guide that would help several different audiences and add value to the already-crowded project management, problem-solving, and consulting fields of literature? While this book was theoretically similar to *The McKinsey Mind* at the start, I hope that it will add specificity and tips that will benefit current consultants, executives working in teams, and students and faculty in top academic institutions by offering some guidelines, checklists for projects, and illustrations of tools and templates for more high-impact deliverables.

My military observations developed primarily over the past year as I delivered several workshops to consulting firms on this approach to team problem solving. One day, while on vacation in the beautiful mountains of North Carolina (I am so glad that my wife, Meredith, comes from such an amazing area), I happened to come across a special program on the History Channel that was entitled "The Complete History of the Green Berets." In addition, the Army conducts much of its Green Berets training in North Carolina. The depiction of how the Green Berets were founded and how they go about their training, revealed some amazing similarities to those experienced at McKinsey. Everything—the core values, clear missions, consistency in techniques, and significant investments in training and world-class results—mapped across both organizations. The more I researched the special forces organization and its training, the more parallels came to light. I even borrowed the terms Rules of Engagement and Operating Tactics in my organizing framework.

THE APPROACH

During my journey to create a team problem-solving "Master Guide of SOPs (Standard Operating Procedures)," the goal of making a high-impact contribution was paramount. After developing a formal set of Rules of Engagement for top projects, the concepts were tested through training programs, secondary research, and more than 100 interviews with consultants. Training programs were created and delivered to students, faculty, executives, and consultants; each session focused on pragmatic, actionable tactics for successful project management. Also included in the approach was research on books on project management, consulting, and strategic thinking. My most valuable sources of input were conversations with current and former consultants from McKinsey and other top firms who graciously listened to my ideas and shared their own thoughts, stories, and anecdotes.

What did I learn during this process? A few key takeaways come to mind. First, the concepts are *not rocket science*. Very little in this book is complex, new, or revolutionary. That having been said, the value proposition of the thoughts presented herein (and my motivation for continuing with the book-writing effort) is the organization of the concepts, prioritization of implementation considerations, and real-life examples that should bring the ideas to life. Also, the templates and tools will save teams time as they work to use the concepts in their projects.

Second is the critical importance of *discipline in execution*. The more one analyzes the success that McKinsey continues to enjoy year after year (and the success of organizations such as the Green Berets), the more it is apparent that such success stems from consistent delivery of a clearly articulated sense of values and protocols. I have observed similar concepts in discussions and training programs in many other consulting firms, but very few of these firms have achieved the level of project management excellence (referred to here as "team problem solving," as it is a bit broader than just managing the project) and continued impact throughout the world that McKinsey has (working for the vast majority of the Fortune 100 companies in the world). One of the key elements enabling this discipline is massive investment in recruiting, bringing people on board, training, mentoring, and rewarding people for the desired behaviors that McKinsey has identified as being critical for success.

Finally, *good consultants must understand and excel at the art of storytelling*. Among other things, a good story can help to hold people's attention, to build an interpersonal connection, and to persuade an audience. This concept is built into the model discussed here, and its contribution to successful completion of this project is signficant. In addition to sharing stories (good and bad) from top consultants about their implementation of many of the ideas from this book, a team of MBA students volunteered to work on a pro bono project to apply the tools, to document the results, and to tell the implementation story of a real-life engagement. Our approach to this project involved testing a hypothesis about the most important tools for project management and seeking confirming and disconfirming evidence from people who do this for a living (and from students learning the art). What follows is the latest iteration of a model inspired by my experiences at McKinsey but amplified after years of reflection. I hope you find it helpful!

INTRODUCTION

THE MODEL

I would like to introduce you to the TEAM FOCUS model, first describing the ideas at a high level here, then going into much more detail later in the book (each element has its own chapter). In each section, you will find a core concept, detailing a clear and straight-forward set of SOPs (Standard Operating Procedures) with the following five parts:

- Concept: a brief overview of the chapter topic
- Rules of Engagement: three high-priority, action-oriented recommendations
- Operating Tactics: very specific tactical advice
- Stories from the Field: applications and insights from ex-McKinsey consultants and business school students
- Case Study: a true story of how the ideas were implemented during a pro bono consulting project

The concepts are captured by two acronyms that I believe emphasize the model's most critical elements and, more important, capture the essence of the model's two key components. The framework for the book is TEAM FOCUS, which is described here. Note that you will not find the TEAM FOCUS acronym in the training manuals of McKinsey. In the creation of this model, my starting point was the documentation of the key takeaways from my research and experience at McKinsey and other consulting firms that related to team problem solving. Over the past six years, I have been refining the model in pursuit of a framework that summarizes what I feel are the most important concepts for success in this arena. Thus, while the actual framework is not used at McKinsey, the concepts are consistent with those taught to the up-and-coming advisors to the top corporations in the world at McKinsey and elsewhere.

Interpersonal   *Analytical*

Talk   Frame

Evaluate   Organize

Assist   Collect

Motivate   Understand

                         Synthesize

Figure I-1   TEAM FOCUS Model

The first component covers four key elements of the *interpersonal* interactions that affect project management and team problem solving; thus the key word *TEAM*:

TALK—One of the most important elements of high-quality team problem solving is establishing very clear channels of communication. This chapter discusses special communication tools and provides guidance concerning best-process communication, inclusion of important constituents outside of the core team, and tips on managing interpersonal dialogue. The chapter also features a special section about listening.

EVALUATE—Teamwork is a dynamic process, and the most successful teams are those that are able to assess their current level of performance and adapt accordingly. The starting point for good evaluation is an open dialogue about expectations, group norms, specific work processes, and tools for monitoring progress. Implicit in the team evaluation process is an individually based personal plan that allows each team member to grow and develop on a continual basis. We all have strengths and weaknesses, and evaluation is the only way in which we can adequately identify where to focus our energy for improvement.

ASSIST—Once the evaluation process is underway, the next critical phase of the teamwork process is assisting others to complete the team's objectives. This builds on the Evaluate phase, which identifies particular strengths of team members that can be leveraged for the good of the team. Strategic leverage of unique capabilities is an underlying component of all "special forces" organizations and is just common sense. At the same time, team members must hold one another accountable for their assigned responsibilities. Direct, honest, and timely feedback will ensure that the Assist process is operating correctly.

MOTIVATE—The last element of the model's interpersonal component involves very specific strategies for motivation. One of the most important considerations is the realization that team members are motivated by different factors. Accordingly, engaging in informal, candid conversations at the beginning of the project about what those unique motivators are and paying close attention to individuals' drivers will go a long way. Similarly, the best teams are those that provide positive recognition for individual contributions and take adequate time to celebrate as a group (many of us seem to do less and less of this the older we get).

The second component of the model relates to the core *analytical* elements of successful project management. The word itself is conveniently right on target: *FOCUS*.

FRAME—The first element in the FOCUS component is widely regarded as the most important in the entire model. Essentially, framing the problem (*before you begin extensive data collection!*) involves identifying the key question that you are studying, drawing issue trees for potential investigation, and developing hypotheses for testing during the project. Good framing translates into more effective problem solving, as you will be ensuring that the work you are doing will translate into high-impact results—the ultimate measure of effectiveness.

ORGANIZE—This element is a boring but necessary step in preparing the team for efficient problem solving. All teams organize in some manner or another, but my research suggests that more efficient teams organize around content hypotheses with the end in mind. Unfortunately, in many cases, there seems to be a default approach that compels teams to organize quickly around the buckets that seem to surface most easily, rather than on the basis of potential answers to the key question under study.

COLLECT—The next element of the model provides guidance that leads to the collection of relevant data, avoiding the overcollection of data that are not useful. The most efficient teams are those that can look at the two piles of data collected and smile as they realize that the relevant data (pile 1) far outweigh the irrelevant information (pile 2) because the team continuously analyzed the difference.

UNDERSTAND—As the team gathers data, these data must be evaluated for their potential contribution to proving or disproving the hypotheses. At McKinsey, the term used on an almost daily basis is "so what?"—what is the meaning of the insight from these data for the project, and ultimately for the client?

SYNTHESIZE—The final element in the model is to synthesize the information into a compelling story. Here is where the well-known "pyramid principle" related to organizing a written report or slide deck comes into play. In this chapter, I cover the guidelines for putting together and delivering a great final product.

MARCHING FORWARD

This is a guidebook for action. Each chapter builds the toolkit—tool by tool. The goal is to have all team members review the contents before starting a project, then dig deeper into the chapters over the course of the project. The book can also be used in academic settings to teach team problem solving, consulting, or project management. Courses with any sort of field study or consulting project may be able to immediately apply the concepts and templates contained herein. Each chapter concludes with a first-person account of how the tools worked in a real engagement (our case study).

The case study is a key aspect of this book. While I lived these principles during my years at PricewaterhouseCoopers and McKinsey and reflected on them during my years of teaching them to students, it was important to put them to the test in a live engagement. Six students surfaced who were willing to work on a pro bono project with me as a learning and résumé-building experience. One of these students, Tim Krzywicki, will tell you more about it throughout the book as the "narrator" of the team's experiences.

THE CASE STUDY

My name is Tim Krzywicki, and I am a first-year MBA student at the Kelley School of Business at Indiana University. I have been asked to recount my experience utilizing the TEAM FOCUS model while working on a pro bono consulting engagement with Dr. Friga. I'd like to begin by giving you an overview of the project, providing the team members' backgrounds, and then finally explaining how this case study will unfold throughout *The McKinsey Engagement.*

My team was charged with the task of conducting research and issuing recommendations about the strategic plan of an unincorporated area in Johnson County, Indiana, known informally as Center Grove. Specifically, we examined three options for Center Grove: 1) incorporating as an independent entity, 2) inviting annexation by another neighboring town, and 3) doing nothing.

My team members and I volunteered (somewhat unwittingly) to work on this project both for the opportunity to get some real-life experience and also to have a real impact on the community. It was immediately clear to me that this project would be different from a standard business consulting engagement because it was addressing a public issue; however, this interesting dynamic also gave us the potential to affect an entire community. Adding to the unique nature of this engagement was the fact that the project had been initiated by a previous year's group of MBA students, so we were neither jumping onto a project nor starting one from scratch. Rather, we had to pick up the pieces and charge ahead, reviewing dormant and somewhat haphazard research with our eyes firmly fixed on our already-established final deadline: a presentation to key stakeholders at a town meeting in four months.

Our "superstar" team (bear in mind that Dr. Friga seems to call everybody a superstar) consisted of five MBA students—Alan,

Bhavin, Rachita, Shalini, and me—and was headed by Dr. Friga as our engagement partner. We also had special contributions from Chris Cannon, a second-year MBA student who filled the role of engagement manager and is now serving the country as an Army officer in Afghanistan. At the time of the project, I was in my second year of Indiana University's joint JD and MBA program, but I was in my first year at the Kelley School of Business. My eclectic studies also include an undergraduate degree in engineering, so I provided broad knowledge as well as valuable nonbusiness expertise. Even without my multiple fields of study, however, the group members' talents were well balanced. Alan's background was in general management and finance, Bhavin had multiple degrees in computer information systems and information technology, Rachita had engineering and finance concentrations and was consequently quantitatively focused, and Shalini's unique contributions were marketing insight and a truly international perspective (she had lived in six countries and spoke five languages!). There were certainly overlaps of experience within our group, but our backgrounds and especially our interests were diverse enough to provide many perspectives and to help us to be creative as well as effective.

At the end of each chapter, I'll provide my insights into how the key points from that chapter's Rules of Engagement and Operating Tactics applied to our project. Keep an eye out for documents and charts, as I'm also including some of our team's relevant deliverables. You'll see that my reflections are hardly exhaustive; I've chosen to highlight the important points that best show how the framework functions in a real-life project. I'll be honest: some of our experiences were extremely positive, while others are most kindly described as less than neutral. Similarly, we used many of Dr. Friga's Operating Tactics, but we didn't use them all. Ours was not a perfect project, and we certainly ran into our share of obstacles; however, the Johnson County case study was a huge success, and from what I understand, it continues to have lasting impact in the community. More important for your purposes, though, it provides an arena where you can view the strategies and tools detailed in each chapter in a practical light, prodding you to think about what a successful implementation of your next project might look like. I hope that through this real-life application of the TEAM FOCUS framework, you will learn from both our bursts of (brief) brilliance and our mistakes.

Part 1

TEAM

1

TALK

Interpersonal   *Analytical*

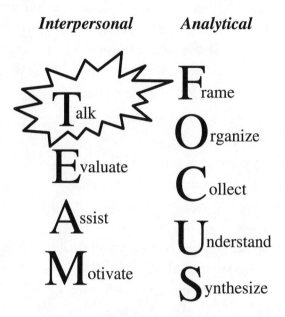

Figure 1-1   TEAM FOCUS Model—Talk

CONCEPT

We begin our journey of dissecting and improving team problem solving with the most obvious, but in my mind the most important and often troublesome, element of team interaction—talking. In fact, during my research and interviews with McKinsey alumni, the Talk element of the model was consistently ranked the most important of all interpersonal elements. Why is it that the simple act of talking can cause so many problems in team problem solving? Generally, because we don't have specific Rules of Engagement; because we like to speak more often than we listen; and because we get personally attached to our own points of view. The good news is that there are a few minor adjustments that can go a long way toward improving the communication among team members—and that is what this chapter aims to provide.

Think of your last major team problem-solving effort and reflect upon the communication process that took place. Specifically, try to answer the following questions:

- Did you ever have a problem tracking down the contact information for a team member?
- Did any team members contribute in a less-than-meaningful way in any team meetings?
- Was there any evidence of redundant work or rework during the project?
- Did any team members ever try to stick to a particular perspective a bit too long?
- Were some of the meetings ineffective, or did any of them end without specific and clear action steps?

Even if you can't remember particular instances in which you encountered these particular issues, this chapter's tips may help you communicate more effectively in your next problem-solving adventure.

RULES OF ENGAGEMENT

Based on observations at McKinsey and on conversations with hundreds of current and former McKinsey consultants, I quickly realized that the issue of communication is a high priority for the firm. While it is not as glamorous as developing the killer recommendation that turns a project around, it is just as important. As tedious as a discussion of communication techniques may seem, it is an important starting point for this book for a reason. The rules of talking (or, more broadly, communicating) are a great place to start, as they constantly affect everyone on the project—far more than any other aspect of team problem solving that I will present in this book.

In each chapter of this book, three key Rules of Engagement will be offered that are designed to provide specific explanations of the primary element of the TEAM FOCUS model discussed in that chapter. Each of the Rules of Engagement is followed by specific Operating Tactics to help you implement these principles in your next engagement. Finally, each chapter concludes with a few stories from my research that illustrate good or bad examples of how these rules can affect team problem solving.

RULE 1: COMMUNICATE CONSTANTLY

Let's do some very loosely defined math for this discussion. I would like to compare the costs of over- vs. undercommunication. First, consider the costs of overcommunication:

- Time to write additional update reports or e-mails
- Time to read additional update reports or e-mails
- Annoyance of yet another e-mail or voice mail update (how many do you receive a day?)

Next, consider the potential costs of undercommunication:

- Lack of other (perhaps divergent) perspectives on important issues

- Redundancy of work streams (people working on the same things)
- The wrong answer or a significant reworking of the analytical process

Which of these strike you as potentially "costing" more (i.e., more risk to a project team)? It seems clear (at least to me) that the costs of undercommunication far exceed those of overcommunication. Thus, we arrive at our first Rule of Engagement: communicate constantly. This policy is applicable throughout the duration of a project; each team member should share information regarding personal background, project background, similar projects, conversations, issues, deliverables, takeaways, new ideas, scope changes, and client input. This includes both good news and bad news (especially bad news, as this is the news that is most likely to require input and adjustment). Much of this communication can take place via e-mail, which has the positive characteristic of being documented for later reference. However, it is better to balance e-mail with phone and in-person communications, as e-mail can often lead to misinterpretation, and these other forms of communication can go a long way toward fostering team harmony and creating clear communication. A good friend of mine (Bill Gilliland) who worked in consulting for a long time always had daily "flash meetings" with his teams, during which they could hit the high points of the project and share insights. This was particularly important with tight deadlines (are there ever loose deadlines?).

RULE 2: LISTEN ATTENTIVELY

I find it quite interesting that although listening skills are generally considered one of the most important sets of skills for executives and consultants, formal courses in listening are uncommon in

MBA and undergraduate management education. In my case, one particular weakness that continues to gnaw at me—and some of you may suffer from it as well—is cutting people off in the middle of their sentences. I like to think it is because I am smart enough to figure out where they are going, but indeed it is just rude! A critical Rule of Engagement is for everyone on the team to learn how to listen attentively.

McKinsey provides specific training on how to become a better listener. It advocates a number of techniques in this area, and four specific tips stand out to me as worthy of repeating:

- Let go of your own agenda—at least for the time being—and don't interrupt.
- Focus on the speaker. Physically look at the speaker, maintain eye contact, and give him or her your undivided attention.
- Encourage the speaker, both verbally and nonverbally (e.g., through body language).
- Discuss the content. Summarize it, paraphrase it, and demonstrate understanding of it.

One more idea related to listening is to actively solicit opinions and ideas from those on a team who have not yet contributed. This is especially important for the quieter or more introverted members of the team.

RULE 3: SEPARATE ISSUES FROM PEOPLE

The final Rule of Engagement under Talk is one of the most effective guidelines for creating team harmony, and it is especially useful when group members are wrestling with tough analytical issues. I imagine everyone reading this book has experienced what I call "he said, she said." Over the course of a team problem-solving effort, there are usually differences of opinion that result from diversity within the team and that contribute to better answers. That is not the problem; the real issue is how we deal with the divergent opinions. The problem is that more often than not, when we put forward an idea or point of view, we become personally attached to that perspective. If our idea is rejected by the group, we may feel an urge to argue more vehemently to get others to accept it. The better approach is to present an idea, separate the person from the idea, and then move to discussing the pros and cons of the idea on its merits only.

OPERATING TACTICS

As discussed earlier, each chapter will conclude with a set of specific Operating Tactics that may help with the implementation of the Rules of Engagement in your respective team problem-solving engagements. While these tactics are basic, my premise is that if your team uses each Operating Tactic shown in this and the subsequent chapters, it will be more effective and efficient than would have been the case otherwise.

The Operating Tactics for the Talk element of the TEAM FOCUS model are:

- *Tactic 1*: Document and share all contact information for the entire internal and external team, identify the key communication point players (who will contact whom), and define the overall scope of the project.
- *Tactic 2*: Agree on a meeting schedule that matches the nature of the project, but try to meet in person as a full team at least weekly (include the client in some meetings), or daily for one- to two-week projects.
- *Tactic 3*: All meetings should have a clear agenda (or list of issues to discuss), produce specific deliverables, and result in new action plans.

- *Tactic 4*: Use e-mail frequently to keep the team updated on progress, and use a brief and consistent format. Remember that overcommunication is better than undercommunication.
- *Tactic 5*: When evaluating the pros and cons of issues and ideas, remember to separate the issue or idea from the person (once an issue or idea is presented, everyone evaluates it on its merit without any personal attachment to it).

STORIES FROM THE FIELD

STORY FROM THE FIELD—1

Topic: One lagging work stream fails to communicate crucial information. A story from a management consultant who worked for two leading global consulting firms in Asia demonstrates that no matter how well a project's other aspects go, poor communication can reduce the team's overall efficiency and lessen its final impact.

During an engagement for a Fortune 500 company in the consumer goods segment, I worked on a project for the company's Japanese subsidiary. The subsidiary was losing market share in Japan, and this loss was believed to be the result of increased low-cost competition. We framed the key question well: why is the company losing market share? From there, we decided to focus on the cost part of our issue tree. Cost was made up of two components: in-plant cost (in the country of manufacture) and cross-country cost (logistics and other shipping-related costs). Having narrowed our focus, we divided ourselves into three subgroups:

- A team focusing on the in-country costs in Japan (basically, the cost of distribution once the product was imported into Japan)

- A team looking at the cost structure of the products manufactured in China and Thailand (this was my team)
- A team analyzing the cost structure of the products manufactured in Australia

During the early stages of the engagement, the team used every tool listed later under FOCUS:

- We framed the question.
- We developed a comprehensive issue tree.
- We benchmarked the players in the industry (and found that the competition was using contract manufacturing—manufacturing in the United States and exporting to Japan)

Teams 2 and 3 conducted extensive interviews in China, Thailand, and Australia while collecting benchmarking data. Based on the input of these groups, we felt confident that we had uncovered the core issue. Our analysis suggested that there was a good opportunity to reduce costs by moving a product portfolio from Australia to Thailand.

Manufacturing in China also offered some cost benefits, but since the local market was growing rapidly, we felt that exporting from China to Japan might not be feasible in the long term. All this time, team 1 was focusing on the cost structure in Japan, and although there were periodic conference calls between the three teams, team 1 was behind schedule in its research and its analysis of Japan's local cost structure.

After the in-country cost teams had finished our analysis and had also created our mock-up final deliverables [similar to ghost charts, which will be introduced in Chapter 7—PF], we recommended moving some products from Australia to

Thailand. Our goal was to reduce the landed cost in Japan and to improve margins as well as market share. But when team 1 finally finished its analysis, the real problem facing the company emerged. The first team found that SG&A costs in Japan were very high. This was due to the fact that the company was run by expatriates from the United States; there were no locals (Japanese) in the management team of the Japanese subsidiary. Some expatriates were costing up to $1 million a year, and it was equally beneficial to reduce the SG&A costs and reduce the cross-country costs.

Team 1's breakdown was driven by both inefficient analysis and communication failure. Whereas teams 2 and 3 utilized the 80/20 rule effectively, team 1 went into too much detail (boiled the ocean); additionally, there was a communication gap between subgroups. These delays in analyzing and communicating the real problem led to project inefficiency, which in turn caused an overall project delay because we had to rework everything. Thus, although we implemented the FOCUS part well, our project was not an overall success because we failed to communicate effectively.

STORY FROM THE FIELD—2

Topic: Multiple teams and time zones lead to inefficient and ineffective communication. Another example that addresses the risks of undercommunication, especially when dealing with issues such as resource allocations and time differences, comes from a consultant at another major consulting firm.

I was part of a major project in Dubai that involved quite a few teams of consultants and other advisors—up to seven at a time—crossing over numerous time zones. In fact, no more than 20 percent of the overall effort participants were in the same time zone at any point in time. In addition to this mix of time zones, the project was complicated by the frequent rotation of team members and leadership of different parties involved.

Some team members laid out best practices that were then shared by other offices, e.g., we began immediately documenting key takeaways after every client or team meeting and sharing them with every team member in real time. It was crucial to maintain 100 percent transparency in communication, as any secrets can have negative effects on team morale and lead to significant delays due to conceptual gaps. We also saw that the larger and more virtual a team becomes, the more means of informal and quick communication need to be encouraged with a high degree of team-oriented proactiveness from all people involved in the effort.

STORY FROM THE FIELD—3

Topic: Clear communication within the team and with external shareholders leads to success.   A colleague of mine described communication as the key element of a successful McKinsey engagement that involved a major North American company sourcing auto parts from low-cost countries.

The background for this project is that the client had spent two years trying to build a sourcing network in low-cost countries, but the project had gained some, but not the desired amount of traction. Several potential reasons for this delay were identified:

- Difficulties holding people accountable
- Difficulties communicating effectively across the organization (both across functions and across geographic areas)
- Need for a louder mandate from senior leadership
- Limited amount of supplier access
- Analytical horsepower

I was part of a 10-person team that stepped in and turned the project around in three months. We delivered an actionable plan that prioritized key obstacles, designed mechanisms for monitoring progress and reviewing opportunities, and obtained buy-in from the client. Two other key deliverables included a robust savings database and comprehensive sourcing toolkit. Some of our keys for successful interactions during the project are outlined here:

- Structure
  - Providing topics for discussion before each meeting and pulling in the key stakeholders meant that meetings tended to be more effective in terms of problem solving and time savings. (Decision meetings were heavily, if not exclusively, fact based.)
  - Structure led to preparation, where attendees could digest the topics and come prepared to ask or field questions.
- Clear communication
  - Straight talk, active listening, and pushing to keep dialogue logically driven steered discussions away from black-and-white, binary, culturally driven responses (e.g., yes or no), and more toward "yes" or "what needs to be done to make the answer yes?"
- Frequency
  - Holding meetings on a regular basis improved overall communication and kept various parts of the organization up to date (especially given team locations in Canada and China).
  - Frequency of meetings with attendees from varying levels in the corporate hierarchy also provided visibility for project owners, a showing of support to the midlevel managers from upper management, and time savings for all parties involved.

Our focus on generating supplier excitement was a specific demonstration of TEAM FOCUS principles, especially the importance of obtaining internal buy-in by cultivating external relationships. Some of my takeaways are given here:

- Show the suppliers the prize by tailoring the presentation to the audience and by giving specific incentives that motivate the audience to action.
- A presentation by senior company executives not only enhances the presentation by showing the sincerity and seriousness of the offer, but also creates structure for the project internally, driving responsible parties inside the company to meet the external commitments (in essence, creating urgency and accountability within the company).

STORY FROM THE FIELD—BUSINESS SCHOOL EXAMPLE

Topic: Communication with constituents leads to support of executive board's plans.   Our first example from the world of business schools comes to us from Columbia. Rob Torti describes a situation that required a significant amount of communication, listening, and separating issues from people:

I had the privilege of serving as the president of the Graduate Business Association (GBA) at Columbia. During my tenure, I remember a project that involved restructuring our organization. The project seemed to be headed for disaster, but it was saved by utilization of some of the tools described in this section. The GBA had an executive leadership team of 12 people, and I was responsible for overall management of the group. It was a diverse group, and it governed all of the different events, academics, finance, community service, IT, clubs, and careers—pretty much everything interacting with students. There were several layers below the executive board, including the student senate, committees, and other clusters. My hypothesis was that there seemed to be duplication of effort and overall poor integration of the different organizations (especially the class committee).

Just as described in the "Separate Issues from People" Rule of Engagement, I presented ideas to the executive board without becoming too attached to the proposals. We had great discussions and came up with a solid plan.

Our breakdown, however, was in the area of communication with the class committee, which would be undergoing the most changes under the proposed plan. When we went public with our ideas, the class committee got very defensive, immediately viewing the plan as being against it and its purpose, rather than being aimed at trying to break down silos and have groups work together better. We made a mistake by not bringing those folks into the discussion early in the process, and the situation got antagonistic, to say the least.

Eventually, we got everyone into the room at the same time, and tempers were pretty high (we didn't need specific approval, but we needed their buy-in to truly implement our ideas). We talked about the process we employed to go through our analysis, our plan, and the need for improvement of the existing structure. When talking about the process, I let all the people involved get their emotions out and vent a little bit, and then we focused on the content (and less on the emotions). It was truly amazing. People weren't set in their ways at all, and they really just came with blank slates. The tone only improved, and we pushed through to come up with a plan that we all approved.

As we were going to roll out our new plan, we ran into the same problem with student clusters and groups (a lot of pushing back, people not being receptive to change). However, we had learned from experience and were more adequately prepared to communicate our plan to other constituents and to secure their support. I certainly have learned some lessons that I plan to implement going forward that relate to communication, active listening, separating issues from people, and the necessity for buy-in during change processes.

CASE STUDY

Hi, it's Tim again. As I mentioned in the introduction, at the end of each chapter, I will be sharing my experiences from a real-life MBA consulting project to show you some examples of the TEAM FOCUS model in action. Here, I have detailed my team's key talk-related practices as well as my own takeaways.

WHAT WE DID

The first things we did to establish a firm foundation of communication within the group were to create a team charter and to work with Dr. Friga to write an engagement memo (see deliverables at the end of the chapter). While the contact information in our team charter was certainly invaluable, the real value-adding contribution of these documents was making sure that everybody was on the same page with regard to expectations, potential issues, goals, and scope.

As far as our communication frequency was concerned, we met weekly to update one another and to work out the project's direction and details, while e-mailing one another occasionally between meetings when it was necessary or helpful. This was a way in which our communication patterns strayed from the strict interpretation of the TEAM FOCUS model—namely, we did not "communicate constantly."

However, it is important to note that our relatively low level of communication was decided upon deliberately and was the result of another unique characteristic of this project: that everybody's parts were mutually exclusive and collectively exhaustive (MECE—see Chapter 5 for more information about the MECE concept), so there was minimal overlap in our work streams. To put it more colloquially, we divided and conquered. Each of us had his or her own (eventually) well-defined subject areas, and our research was relatively independent of other project components. We simply did not need to be in constant contact for most of the project, and daily updates and tedious e-mail strings would have been excessive. However, toward the end of our project, as we were piecing all our research together to create one cohesive story and focusing on collective deliverables as opposed to individual work streams, we met much more frequently as a group.

Regarding our group communication style, we all consciously strove to separate ideas from people; this is one of Dr. Friga's most important tenets of teamwork, and it had been drilled into us already through his classes. This separation of issues from people was contingent upon two abilities. First, we all tried to be somewhat relaxed about our own ideas; not taking ourselves too seriously allowed us to venture our thoughts without becoming too personally invested in them. Second, we made sure to respect other teammates and their suggestions, focusing our discussion and criticism on the merits of the ideas, rather than on people. This free, issue-based discussion style enabled us to debate the issues without being overly worried about offending a team member.

WHAT I LEARNED

It is important to tailor one's communication style and frequency to the project—one standard communication style will not necessarily be appropriate for every project. For example, because our assignments were relatively autonomous, there was not much interdependence between our "bucket" issues. Therefore, we communicated regularly, but spent most of the week working independently. In other projects I've participated in, there has generally been more overlapping of tasks, and therefore more frequent communication is necessary.

This seems like common sense, but in this project, it became apparent that when the project sponsor or partner (in our case, Dr. Friga) is in attendance, team members are generally better prepared and more on task. We found that we gave ourselves much more leeway and were more easily sidetracked when it was just the five of us meeting.

The second point is similar: I learned that when the sponsor or partner is actively engaged with creating the team charter and establishing guidelines, it is easier for team members to focus on the issues instead of attacking personalities. Because Dr. Friga is so adamant about separating ideas from people and had a clear vision of how he wanted the project to be run, it was easy for us to fall in line and internalize his project values as our own.

DELIVERABLES

Team Name	CG2020 (Center Grove 2020)
Client Name	White River Citizens United (and Johnson County commissioners and county council members)
Project Description	Investigate incorporation/annexation options for White River Township in Johnson County, IN
Potential Issues	• Lack of relevant data • Public resistance to ideas
Success Goals	• Clear recommendations that are understandable by the general public and supported by data • Usable document that will be used by the county leaders to make decisions going forward
Guiding Principles	• Employ the tools from the TEAM FOCUS framework • Ensure that all work is high impact

CONTACT INFORMATION

Name	Role	E-mail	Phone (W)	Phone (M)
Dr. Paul Friga	Project Oversight			
Chris Cannon	Project Manager			
Alan Burleson	MBA Consultant			
Tim Krzywicki	MBA Consultant			
Shalini Makkar	MBA Consultant			
Bhavin Shah	MBA Consultant			
Rachita Sundar	MBA Consultant			

Figure 1-2   Talk: Team Charter

CG2020 - Letter of Agreement

Dear Mr. Dorsett,

I am pleased to present the following overview of a proposed pro bono project for the White River Citizens United (and Johnson County leaders). In this letter, I will address our project's scope, timing, and approach, and I certainly welcome your group's input and suggestions.

We understand that the White River Township area of Johnson County is currently unincorporated, and that county leaders have not reached a consensus on the appropriate course of action. We believe that Johnson County has three viable options: to incorporate as an independent city, to invite annexation by a neighboring town or city (e.g., Bargersville or Greenwood), and to do nothing.

The project team will consist of 4–5 MBA students at the Kelley School of Business, who will operate under my supervision (I have attached my CV for your convenience); our objective is to provide an independent perspective regarding Johnson County's options. In seeking to answer whether or not this area should seek to incorporate, we will gather and analyze primary and secondary data including, but not limited to, the following:

- Interviews with key constituents in Johnson County (WRCU members, county commissioners, mayors, etc.)
- Review of previous analysis/reports on this topic and articles written
- Possible comparisons to similar incorporation efforts (in or out of Indiana)

We plan to begin the project in January 2007 (although we may have a few internal meetings in December), and we expect to deliver our report by the end of the semester (May 2007). Our ultimate deliverable will include the following:

- Benefits
- Infrastructure——roads, services, trails, economic development
- Character——development, control
- Costs (both one-time and ongoing)
  - Administrative
  - Legal
  - Physical
- Recommendation and risks/caveats

My team is very excited about making a real impact and helping Johnson County's leaders guide the area's future – I look forward to working with you and I welcome your input.

Consultant
Dr. Paul Friga
Project Coordinator
November 20, 2006

Client
Name: _____
Position: _____
Date: _____

Figure 1-3   Talk: Engagement Letter

2

EVALUATE

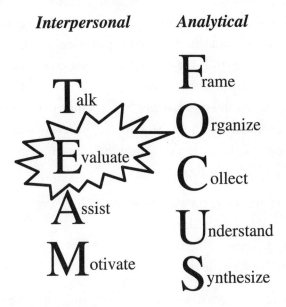

Interpersonal   *Analytical*

Talk   **F**rame

Evaluate   **O**rganize

Assist   **C**ollect

Motivate   **U**nderstand   **S**ynthesize

Figure 2-1   TEAM FOCUS Model—Evaluate

CONCEPT

Once a team has been formed and the rules for communication are established (see Chapter 1), the interpersonal dynamics begin. For this chapter, let's make a general assumption that anyone reading this book has a desire to grow personally and professionally. The bottom line is that we cannot grow very much on our own, and team interactions afford us a tremendous opportunity to achieve that growth.

A crucial element of successful growth in teams is the evaluation element. Just as we may all want to grow, we also recognize that it can be difficult at times ("no pain, no gain"). I have worked on approximately 250 teams over the past 20 years, and the growth was not equal in each team experience. One of the key ingredients of growth is the evaluation of progress toward defined goals, on both a team and an individual basis. When those goals are not specifically enumerated, it can be difficult to measure progress.

The content that must be covered in evaluations is fairly straightforward. In fact, the following key questions drive the guidelines provided in this chapter:

- What are the team members' individual working styles?
- How will we get along?
- Who is responsible for what?
- How is everyone doing?

Sound familiar? I thought so. One value-added area during training at McKinsey and other top consulting firms is the approach to performing the evaluation. To say that you get "adequate" evaluation and feedback is an understatement—if feedback is a "gift" (a common expression at many consulting firms, especially Deloitte), then at consulting firms, it's always your birthday. However, too much evaluation can take a toll on individuals, even if they have a strong growth agenda. Thus, the process of giving constructive feedback that continues to motivate and drive others, as opposed to confidence-breaking criticism, is truly an art.

There are three critical success factors for a good evaluation system within a team (note that we are not discussing overall firm evaluation systems here, although there are certainly similarities):

- *Openness.* All of the team members must have an interest in receiving feedback on their performance.
- *Explicitness.* While evaluative processes are often helpful, there must be explicit conversations about the intent and process of evaluation to make it most effective.
- *Agreement.* Before an evaluation takes place (before any feedback, actually), there should be agreement between the sender and the recipient as to the objectives of the evaluation and the measures for it.

RULES OF ENGAGEMENT

There are three key recommendations for action to facilitate a good evaluation process on any team, and thereby lead to growth of all the team members.

RULE 1: DISCUSS TEAM DYNAMICS

The starting point for a good team evaluation culture is to have an open and casual discussion about the team's use of evaluation tools. At McKinsey, this is a strongly suggested step (in fact it was mandatory) during the team project. It is usually manifested in the form of a kickoff conversation, a midpoint check, and an "after-action" review (although the last phase is sometimes captured in the individual evaluations).

The topics that should be covered are fundamental: the default and preferred working profile and personality of each team member, how to handle disagreements (which will always occur), and how to communicate individual and team progress. The challenge is to convince the entire team that these topics are worthy of discussion. There is often a tendency to avoid these types of conversations, as we all have substantial experience working in teams. The truth of the matter, though, is that the team will enjoy a much more positive working environment just by having the conversation.

In my classes, this lesson is taught by having new teams work on a survival exercise immediately after forming (e.g., if you were stranded in a subarctic locale, how would you prioritize a given set of items?). We then spend a few minutes explaining how critical it is for teams to have an open culture and to discuss the individual styles of the team players, guiding principles, and group objectives. We then take the same pool of students and group them into new teams, reminding them to cover these details quickly (this is a 15-minute exercise) before working on the problem. Without fail, the second teams operate more effectively and efficiently, and the team members usually have a better time working together.

Remember that these conversations should not be overly formal or intense; they just need to happen. This type of explicit conversation controls for individuals' variance in perception, and misperception is one of the most common types of miscommunication. Often, as described in the first "Story from the Field" later in this chapter, the best conversations take place in a casual setting, such as during dinner or over a drink.

RULE 2: SET EXPECTATIONS AND MONITOR RESULTS

The second Rule of Engagement relating to Evaluate involves the more formal steps of setting and documenting expectations and tracking results. Why is this necessary? Because you get what you measure. This is true in business and in team processes. In this case, however, it is less about quantitative measures of effectiveness and more about task completion.

One of the most common errors related to setting and monitoring expectations involves "telling" vs. "asking." I learned this distinction early in my career at PricewaterhouseCoopers when dealing with administrative support staff. Under the pressures of a project, certain people (like me) may have a default tendency to shift to a more authoritarian tone and to assign tasks quickly so that they can get back to more "important" work. The risk in a professional setting (including business schools—especially when dealing with peer teams) is that the recipient of the "order" may not understand, agree with, or eventually complete the assignment.

A better approach is to set expectations jointly. The starting point is to agree on what tasks are necessary in order to accomplish the team's objectives, and also to come to a consensus on the order in which these tasks must occur. Everyone should see how each piece contributes to the overall success of the team. Next, the team divides the tasks (based upon experience, expertise, and/or interest), and each person begins to "own" a particular piece of the project. Then, each person should offer an idea as to the specific deliverable (format and timing). The tasks and expectations should be documented and tracked; this helps to ensure transparency and to see that the loads are divided among all team members equitably based upon their respective roles. Tracking the results and revising the plans becomes much easier if this process is followed, and team members will be more motivated when they know how their contribution fits in and that others will be watching for the completion of their assignments.

RULE 3: DEVELOP AND REEVALUATE A PERSONAL PLAN

The final rule of engagement is a mandate for the explicitness of the personal growth objective that I assume each person on a team possesses (note that I am not naïve enough to think that each person on every team is motivated primarily by personal growth opportunities, but I imagine that most of us are generally trying to grow). The rule calls for each one of us to do an honest assessment of our current strengths and weaknesses as we enter a particular team project and to *share* the key findings with the other members of our team.

First, the assessment. Each of us has unique strengths and weaknesses, and the team environment is a wonderful opportunity to use our strengths to help others and to work with others to improve the areas where we are weak (notwithstanding the current movement to forget your weaknesses and concentrate on your strengths, which actually does have some validity). The key is to do an honest assessment, which can be difficult, as we are often overconfident. I am reminded of a landmark study done in the 1970s in which 1 million students were surveyed and 70 percent of those surveyed placed themselves above average in terms of leadership (not likely possible, is it?). Given this tendency to overconfidence, the key to an honest assessment is to rely on others whose opinions you trust and who would have a basis for reaching a valid conclusion.

Just as a company does a SWOT (Strengths, Weaknesses, Opportunities, and Threats) analysis as part of its strategy development, you can compare yourself against your peers in terms of development opportunities. The key is to find an opportunity for development on this new project. Some questions to consider are:

- How well do I listen?
- Do I get my points across in a nonconfrontational way?
- Do I separate issues from people?

- Do I work independently too much and leave the team in the dark?
- Do I never work independently of the team?
- Do I make people comfortable discussing ideas with me?
- Do I follow through on my commitments?
- Is my work generally error-free?

Next, the sharing. Once you identify a key development opportunity for yourself on a given project, you should share that information with the team. Yes, many of us may prefer to keep it to ourselves (not too many of us like to have our weaknesses exposed), but this is a critical step to team harmony—a component that I refer to as the "humility factor." Have you worked with individuals who were extremely intelligent, but not good team members? What I have found is that the team members who really seem to believe that they don't have any weaknesses are the hardest to engage. Not only are they less open to negative feedback, but they make you feel as if you don't have as much to contribute.

On the other hand, have you worked with people who have a lot to offer, but are aware of their limitations (and are not afraid to mention them)? Isn't it a bit easier to work with them? In my mind, they exhibit the humility factor, which is an important ingredient for team harmony. Just the mere act of admitting something that each person is working on can dramatically affect the way the team gets along. This is why it is recommended that each person do his or her own assessment prior to beginning a project, then share something that he or she is working on improving and ask for the group's help in making progress. It is then up to each individual to track his or her progress, to seek input, and to reevaluate actions taken toward making the desired improvements.

OPERATING TACTICS

The Operating Tactics for the Evaluate element of the TEAM FOCUS model are:

- *Tactic 6*: Identify the personality types of the team members (including the client).
- *Tactic 7*: Hold a brief, relaxed session at the outset of the project to discuss personalities and working preferences. Keep the dialogue open over the course of the project.
- *Tactic 8*: Be aware of your default tendencies, but incorporate the flexibility to deal with different personality types as needed.
- *Tactic 9*: Each team member should identify and document his or her one or two primary objectives in the project.
- *Tactic 10*: The team should openly discuss and reconcile individuals' personal objectives.
- *Tactic 11*: Establish procedures for handling disagreements and giving and receiving feedback.
- *Tactic 12*: Hold regular feedback sessions to allow time for improvement.

STORIES FROM THE FIELD

STORY FROM THE FIELD—1
Topic: Team dynamics discussion simplifies cross-cultural project management.   Our first story from the field comes from D. A. Gros, a former associate principal with McKinsey who is now a vice president at an investment bank. D. A. recalls the importance

of the first Rule of Engagement, "Discuss Team Dynamics," which affected a project he was running out of Chicago.

> We were working on a six- to eight-week product strategy project for a pharmaceutical company that was based in France, for which the deliverables would be entirely in French. The project brought together consultants from geographically, culturally, and linguistically diverse backgrounds—this is increasingly common in the firm. The members included:
>
> - A junior engagement manager from Paris (originally from rural southern France)
> - An associate from New Jersey (physician who spoke no French)
> - A Spanish associate who was an ex-investment banker and had a working command of French
> - A partner from France (Ph.D. in science)
> - A partner from New Jersey (MBA who spoke no French)
>
> Clearly, we had our hands full in terms of handling the diversity of backgrounds, especially given the short time frame of the project. From day one, the team got off to a great start. We met in the McKinsey Paris office and covered the structure and the approach for the project. After discussing the project details in the office, we headed out to a bistro on the Champs-Elysées to discuss team dynamics, including self-introductions, individual work styles, Myers-Briggs, and so on. I knew that this step would be very important to ensure that the team members would get along, learn from one another, and deliver on high expectations. Each person had a critical role in the process, and we had to spend some time getting to know each other and the roles we would play on the project.

STORY FROM THE FIELD—2

Topic: A change in team size and structure necessitates a new "evaluation" plan.   Our second story from the field comes from ex-McKinsey consultant Yannick Grecourt, now with Deutsche Bank in Belgium, who vividly remembers the role of evaluation in a team project and the importance of explicit conversations.

> The situation was a new engagement for a client. The team started with only an engagement manager and one associate, but after two months the team had increased and now consisted of an engagement manager and six other consultants. The complication was that the Evaluate plan had been done at the start of the project for a small team, and we hadn't taken the needed time to rediscuss and adapt the plan for a larger team and an increase in the scope of the project (the Evaluate plan was even more important with a six-person team and one EM to steer).
>
> Our resolution was to take a formal step back and organize a team learning exercise. Such an exercise is often better if it is led by someone outside the team to discuss the three main points of Evaluate. Each of us could share his or her point of view on group dynamics, discuss learning and development opportunities, and get to know one another better. The team became much more effective after some crucial points were discussed. Specifically, there was some jealousy because the EM was sharing a room with one junior associate, who consequently had more access to him than the rest of the team. Also, there was a lack of understanding about some work-stream delegation decisions—some of the choices had been made by the client, as he was already used to working with a specific consultant. We resolved these and other misunderstandings with open discussions.

STORY FROM THE FIELD—3

Topic: Disclosing personal weaknesses leads to personal improvement and team success. Our final story from the field is a clear articulation of how admitting a development opportunity may have made life easier for a consultant. Victoria Lim, now an associate director at UBS in Singapore, remembers how it took her a while to communicate a personal learning objective on her first project at McKinsey.

> I remember my first McKinsey engagement, when one of my personal goals was to hone my skills in Microsoft Excel. As part of this engagement, my EM asked me to perform various analyses on the client's customer data to help the team understand the dynamics of the client's customer base. There was a huge amount of data that cut across different segments, products, and years. Because of my limited proficiency in Excel, I was doing most of the calculations manually, and any small change to the data set meant hours of extra work. My EM couldn't understand why I took such a long time to make any changes, and I didn't know how to manage expectations. Finally, one of my other team members stepped in to take a look at the monster I had created in Excel, and promptly sat down (at 3 a.m.) to coach me for two hours. I've since learned that it is better to discuss learning objectives early, to ask for help before spinning my wheels, and to manage others' expectations—these all help me grow individually and contribute to team success.

STORY FROM THE FIELD—BUSINESS SCHOOL EXAMPLE—1

Topic: A business school leader discusses group dynamics and the importance of feedback. Clifford Dank, the MBA Association president at the Haas School of Business (University of California at Berkeley), discusses how taking the time to get to know one another informally lays the groundwork for a successful and pleasant group experience. He also explains the evolution of his executive board, which started as a group of distinct individuals, swung to the other extreme and fell into groupthink, then found the happy medium.

> As the president of the MBA Association, I lead a team of 12 vice presidents with varied backgrounds—they are diverse in age, geographical orientation, and culture. They are functionally diverse as well, as each vice president deals with a separate and unique issue (e.g., academics, diversity, or corporate relations). Initially, I thought it was going to be very difficult for us to function as one cohesive unit, and I was very dedicated to finding a way to make us a real team, not just a group of people with similar job titles. At the beginning, we definitely overdid it—we were so focused on being team-oriented that we constantly fell into groupthink and strove to have a consensus on all issues. However, as we matured and grew more confident in our roles, we understood that the value that each of us brings to the team is based on that person's own unique perspectives. We evolved throughout our first semester to become a well-run group, in which we were comfortable expressing our own thoughts, but also respected individual decision makers and trusted them enough not to micromanage and constantly proofread each other's work.
>
> In order to define group goals, objectives, and dynamics, we started the semester with a retreat. We aligned our goals there, and discussed what we as a group represented to the student body. We did not have much discussion about specific

objectives, as most of our work was done autonomously or with our own subgroups. However, because we had defined our goals, we were able to make sure that our own individual objectives contributed to the group's overall mission. To establish positive group dynamics, I used improvisational comedy icebreakers as a starting point to allow us to get a feel for the different members' personalities; I found this to be very effective, as all the participants seemed to shed their shells and enjoy themselves. At the retreat we also answered different personality-type questions very informally—in lieu of the standard Myers-Briggs test, we asked each other interesting questions (e.g., "What is your greatest hope and your greatest fear?").

Our group was very feedback-oriented, which is a natural result of going to a very feedback-focused school. For example, we have a whole class geared toward incorporating constructive feedback as a cornerstone of effective communication (I teach this class as a professor's assistant). I think this is a great component of our program, as it is one of the most applicable things we learn: if you cannot communicate your thoughts effectively to both peers and superiors in a feedback-type setting, you won't be an effective leader. I incorporated feedback in the executive board by having each person fill out a feedback form for everybody else on the team after three months of working together. Although this was somewhat tedious (filling out 12 evaluations!), at the end of the day, everybody thought it proved useful. To get feedback from the student body, I sent an e-mail to everybody in the business school asking for feedback on the student government (95 out of 480 people responded). We have been striving to incorporate this feedback as we reexamine our goals and objectives.

STORY FROM THE FIELD—BUSINESS SCHOOL EXAMPLE—2

Topic: A team surmounts cultural differences by discussing work styles and setting ground rules.   A germane example comes to us from a second-year MBA student at the University of Michigan's Ross School of Business, who discusses an experience in which teammates' cultural differences led to a misunderstanding of work and communication styles. By discussing these differences openly, the team was able to adapt its plans and establish some ground rules, drastically improving team dynamics.

> I was on a class team assigned to analyze marketing practices and develop a marketing campaign. Our team was very culturally diverse (with members from Russia, India, and the United States), and these cultural differences invariably influenced our working styles. A misunderstanding of these differences caused friction in the team at times. Most notably, the more direct people tended to clash with those of us who are more subtle in their communication style. To compound this difficulty, most of us were type A individuals who weren't naturally very good listeners.
>
> For example, at one point, we were supposed to e-mail the professor a component of our project by midnight. At 11:59, we were ready to send the e-mail, and the atmosphere was understandably tense. Because of my cultural upbringing, I considered it unacceptable to send an e-mail to a professor without including a courteous message. I took the time to compose a polite e-mail despite our time crunch, and several team members were understandably annoyed and frustrated.
>
> We dealt with these issues by talking about them openly. We were all in a class about managing teams, so we readily

recognized that we had significant cultural differences. Each of us explained his or her own cultural customs and practices, and then we discussed how we could work together and communicate better; specifically, we decided to give each other more space and to rely on delegation more. Despite one teammate who never really came into the fold, our team really came together in the end.

CASE STUDY

Hi, Tim here. As we set out to implement the Evaluate ideas in our case study, we thought it would be a piece of cake. We were wrong. Peer-based teams can make role assignments and evaluation difficult at times. Let me explain.

WHAT WE DID

We were very conscious of the need to assign roles and responsibilities carefully, and so we spent a long time at the beginning of the project deciding how we would divide the project into buckets (see Chapter 6). Once this initial brainstorming and structuring was completed, though, we were not able to call it a day; we monitored these buckets constantly throughout the project, reevaluating and refining our original structure. Once we came up with our key areas, though, it was relatively simple to assign responsibility. We matched ourselves up with an appropriate bucket based upon background and interest. For example, because of my law background, I volunteered for the "Incorporation/Annexation" category, which covered the legal issues of the project.

Once we each had our assigned roles, we defined our own individual objectives and created our own work plans. We then worked individually throughout the week and shared our results at weekly meetings. One of our first steps was to create "fact packs" containing the most important information about our topic; we then shared this information with the other team members, which helped us to see more and different options and to understand how our components fit into the big picture.

We followed the same sort of process throughout the project, gathering information and forming our own conclusions before offering them to the group for feedback. This group time was particularly important for us because of the high level of autonomy in our own assignments. Throughout the week, we were dealing only with our own small portions of the overall project, and so it would have been very easy to slip into a very narrow view of the project. By paying careful attention to this potential pitfall and by updating one another at weekly meetings, we were able to reconcile our personal objectives with the team's objectives and goals.

WHAT I LEARNED

In the Johnson County study, it became clear that the goals for the team as a whole are easier to define than individual objectives, but that achieving these big-picture goals is much harder than simply throwing together individual research. In any team project, the individual parts are important and contribute to the overall effectiveness; however, the real measure of success is not whether any one component is outstanding, but rather how the overall project turns out.

I also learned that peer-based teams can be difficult to manage. Dr. Friga and Chris Cannon helped with this issue as they stressed specific roles and ownership of the pieces of the project. I also learned how important it is to have a "process-driven" person who keeps things moving forward at all times, but I believe that is covered more in the next chapter.

DELIVERABLES

Name	Tim Krzywicki
Project	Center Grove Incorporation Study
Incoming Strengths and Weaknesses	• Strengths: I have strong analytical abilities, legal knowledge, and work ethic • Weaknesses: I am a bit shy in groups, so I sometimes delay in sharing ideas and hold back in group discussions; I also lack business problem-solving confidence
Development Objectives	• Communication: I plan to push myself out of my comfort zone and speak up more • Knowledge application: I look forward to using my legal knowledge practically • Confidence: I hope to develop business confidence and to trust myself more
Results	Our team really gelled well—because I felt comfortable with the team, I found it easier to contribute my own ideas and to debate others' more. I realized that I really do have a lot to contribute, and I feel much more confident in my abilities.

Figure 2-2   Evaluate: Individual Plan

3

ASSIST

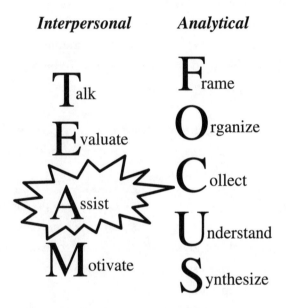

Interpersonal   *Analytical*

Figure 3-1   TEAM FOCUS Model—Assist

CONCEPT

Once the project is up and running, there are a few critical steps that
we can all take to ensure smooth sailing. Speaking of sailing, for illus-
trative purposes let's envision a sailing adventure with my wife, you,

and anyone else you wish to bring. We are going to take a Sunfish, which is a very small sailboat, the type that my brother, father, and I sailed on lakes and rivers growing up in Virginia. We must discuss our approach before boarding and agree on what each of us is going to be responsible for. All four of us must play a role and be ready to help each other out over the course of the three-hour tour. Meredith can handle the rudder; I will deal with the sails. One of you will handle the anchor, and the other can focus on leaning to either side to provide extra weight. And by the way, there will be times when each of us will have to help someone else, should the weather turn or the wind shift dramatically, so be ready to be flexible (plus a little variety makes it more interesting). We must be ready to assist.

Experience and research suggest that there are typically three key areas where issues arise related to providing adequate assistance during a team problem-solving project.

- *Confusion over roles.* The most common problem is that after the team is formed, assignments are doled out very quickly, without giving much thought to everybody's capabilities and interests—a common mentality is to "just divide this up and get started."
- *Feedback not provided (or not provided well).* If any of us really want to develop and grow, we need to receive feedback. The problem is that we don't really want to hear about our weaknesses (these days it seems like we prefer to call these "opportunities for improvement"), or, more important, the messages are delivered in an awkward or personal way that makes them hard to digest.
- *Overfocus on our own assignments.* We all tend to prioritize our tasks based upon maximizing the benefits to ourselves, and as a result, we often lose sight of whether or not our teammates need help.

RULES OF ENGAGEMENT

I have formulated three key recommendations to facilitate a good assistance process on any team, one that will lead to the growth of all the members on a team and increased team effectiveness.

RULE 1: LEVERAGE EXPERTISE

This Rule of Engagement builds on discussing strengths and weaknesses, the importance of which was detailed in the previous chapter. It should be a "no-brainer" for teams to take advantage of the inherent expertise of their members, but for some reason that doesn't always happen. Often, we just don't take the time to ask what our team members' strengths are, or perhaps we focus more on what people want to work on at that particular time than on their capabilities. You have to (or should) take an inventory of team members' skills (what they have done) and wills (what they would like to do), and have an explicit conversation about assignments. In essence, do an assessment based upon the respective education, work experience, and personal experience of everyone on the team.

Consulting firms do this in a very scientific way, using electronic databases to provide data on skills and availability that are useful in creating deployment strategies. Even if you are on a team that was formed without any strategic input, the skills and wills inventory should still be done.

After the inventory, the team should then venture into a "roles" discussion. Who is going to be responsible for what on this project? Generally, high-level roles that people play on teams (especially in business schools) boil down to two categories: process and content.

Process Roles

- *"Big picture person."* This team member focuses on the overall story of the project and the presentation.
- *"Deliverables driver."* This person keeps track of the time and the status of deliverables.
- *"Communicator."* This person is the one primary point of contact with clients.
- *"Devil's advocate."* This team member ensures that alternative views are considered.
- *"Touchy feely."* This is the person who continuously checks the morale of the team.

Content Roles

- *"Functional expert."* People in this role concentrate on strategy, marketing, finance, operations, or some other area.
- *"Relationship guru."* This team member focuses on the relationship with external constituents.
- *"Voice of experience."* This is someone who has worked on a similar project in the past.

Don't forget that there is a chance that no one on the team has an immediate strong content role (this is not likely in a consulting firm, but it is certainly possible on business school teams). In this case, a significant effort must be made to locate some content expertise outside the team. Many times teams, and companies for that matter, default to secondary research rather than holding conversations with experts. I recommend flipping your research plan of attack, first asking others what they know and then using secondary research to fill in the gaps. While you do need to do some basic fact finding as part of every project, conversations with experts will provide significantly more bang for the buck! A final consideration is that, depending upon the size of a team, it is entirely possible that one person will play multiple roles. Just remember to keep the workload equitable.

RULE 2: KEEP TEAMMATES ACCOUNTABLE

One of the paramount operating practices for team members at McKinsey is *ownership*. Ownership means that each person on a team, from the brand-new business analyst to the most senior partner on the engagement, knows the big picture of the project (its mission and objectives) and knows how he or she fits in. Not only is the overall puzzle picture clear, but each person takes ownership of a piece of that puzzle. This is an important concept, because each person on a team should be doing something of value and contributing to the team's overall success (see Chapter 4). The other positive by-product is that the other team members are aware of what each person is working on, what deliverables are anticipated, and when to expect them.

Another major principle within this Rule of Engagement is the importance of deadlines. In Chapter 6, I will describe the use of content and process maps to guide engagements. For now, I think we can all relate to how important deadlines are to getting things done. In fact, deadlines are the backbone of the consulting process, as they give targets for the time by which a certain analysis must be completed. Deadlines also drive efficiency, as there is a tendency to add work to fill the available time; our goal is to force ourselves and our teams to be sure that everything that we are doing is adding value and having an impact on the end product for the client.

Deadlines also give us a chance to reconnect with our teams to review the status of the pieces that each person owns and how the overall story is coming together. Every engagement has a mix of "individual" and "team" time, and the deadlines ensure that we have adequate (but not too much) team time to allow multiple perspectives and inputs for the "ideation." It is also during the team time that we can review the current workload and assignments to ensure that our efforts are equitable and are continuing to contribute in a meaningful way to the overall direction of the project. However, this is a fine line, as we don't want to micromanage the process, and we must trust our teammates to complete their assignments adequately. The Russian proverb that Ronald Reagan was fond of repeating is very fitting in these types of situations: "Trust, but verify."

This leads to my last thought on keeping teammates accountable. Very rarely do we get the key issues, hypotheses, and work streams completely nailed down at the start of a project. In fact, iteration and modification are part of the process described in the second half of this book, the FOCUS section. With that in mind, we should all realize that adjustments of assignments and workloads are to be expected; for some reason, many of the teams I have been on have preferred to try to keep the original course. By shifting assignments a bit based upon their current status of completion and importance to the final story-line creation, we are given an invaluable opportunity to assist our teammates and keep things "sailing" along.

RULE 3: PROVIDE TIMELY FEEDBACK

The final Rule of Engagement of this chapter is dedicated to covering the touchy topic of feedback. Let's face it, every team will have issues, disagreements, and improvement opportunities (just as we all experience personal growth opportunities every day). The best teams are the ones that handle feedback in a constructive and timely fashion. There have been hundreds of books written on this topic, but I would like to distill the concepts that seem to surface as the most important from my experience and research.

The most important aspect of effective feedback is that it must be delivered in a timely manner. This means that we must all share and receive feedback *during* and not just *after* the engagement. Postmortem feedback (especially in terms of after-action reviews) is helpful, but the more meaningful feedback comes during the project. This gives the person receiving the feedback a chance to work on improvement during the life of that particular engagement and minimize the negative effect of whatever the person is not doing well.

Feedback should also generally be done in private. There may be times when a team does a group-sharing session, especially if it is facilitated by a third party. Most of the time, however, feedback is better delivered in private, and it should be presented in a non-threatening and helpful way. The word choice is critical. Here's a great example of how *not* to do this from a particular partner in charge of reorganization consulting at PwC in New York City. After my first week on the project, he took a look at the deliverable and exploded at me in front of several employees in the office. After about 10 minutes of this "feedback," I was more focused on the feedback approach than on the feedback itself. At least he was giving it to me in time to do something about it, rather than just waiting until after the engagement to yell at me.

What should be included in feedback? First, it should be balanced. Feedback should not be limited to the negative aspects of someone's performance on a team (often euphemized as "opportunities for improvement" rather than negative observations). When delivering feedback, be sure to include some praise of a positive contribution before delivering the negative comment. A few recommendations for the feedback process follow:

- Deliver balanced feedback.
- Be specific; don't generalize (e.g., "you are not a good problem solver").
- Report from your perspective, not everyone's (e.g., "I react a certain way when you ...").
- Provide examples of the causation and impact.
- End with a positive outlook and offer ideas for improvement and assistance.

OPERATING TACTICS

The Operating Tactics for the Assist element of the TEAM FOCUS model are:

- *Tactic 13:* First spend at least an hour in a general brainstorming session to openly discuss the problem and key issues to explore (see Chapter 6).
- *Tactic 14:* Be sure to balance the load equitably based upon the estimated number of hours required to complete the tasks. Periodically revisit the assignments after work has begun to ensure that the work distribution continues to be equitable.
- *Tactic 15:* Identify and leverage the specific skill set of each team member (and the firm or the client, if applicable).
- *Tactic 16:* Include at least one or two key status report meetings with the team (and the client) to review findings, data sources, and work streams.
- *Tactic 17:* On a daily basis, provide an update of individual and team progress to assess opportunities to adjust workloads and assignments.

STORIES FROM THE FIELD

STORY FROM THE FIELD—1

Topic: Assisting colleagues—even those on different projects on different continents—is beneficial to the firm as a whole. One of my interviewees suggested that the organizational structure and the reward incentives within McKinsey provide insight into ways in which companies can encourage teamwork and mitigate the bias toward individual incentive programs.

An interesting example related to the Assist bucket is how McKinsey structures its internal reward system. McKinsey pays all partners the same salary globally regardless of location, and consultants are also paid on a global basis. Occasionally, problems arise from an individual incentive perspective, as when clients in a country with lower billing rates (like India) require expertise and advice from a partner in another country with a higher billing rate (like the United States).

The general philosophy within the firm is to provide the best of the firm to each client (if the expertise is available), even if there is a loss in billing rates for the work performed. In essence, the U.S. partner is not penalized; instead, the firm absorbs the difference with a long-term understanding that the benefits to the company served and the firm overall outweigh the short-term loss in transfer pricing. Additionally, partners are expected to spend a percentage of their time assisting other projects, regardless of the location of the client demand. This is not the case at many other consulting firms (some have an "eat what you kill" mentality), and it helps to differentiate McKinsey in a very positive way.

STORY FROM THE FIELD—2

Topic: Leveraging the knowledge of multiple work-stream leaders helps one consultant create a cohesive financial model.   Our second story comes from Victoria Lim, who also provided a story in Chapter 2. In this case, Victoria leveraged expertise by frequently consulting with key leaders of her project's multiple work streams.

> I was working on a huge transformation project with at least five different work streams running in parallel. As fate would have it, I was to work on the financial model (I became more confident in Microsoft Excel with every project, and am now pretty proficient!), which had to take into account specific "levers" and recommendations across all the different work streams. It became critical for me to leverage other teammates in order to understand all the work streams and to represent them accurately in the overall model. I communicated with my teammates frequently in order to update them and to hold them accountable for the inputs they provided. These inputs later translated into measurable targets for the implementation team—by delivering on these targets, the client could achieve the expected financial upside shown in the consolidated financial model.

STORY FROM THE FIELD—3

Topic: Formalizing feedback practices helps to make the process more effective.   Another insightful personal story comes to us from Oliver Personnaz, who is currently with Apax Partners in Paris, France. He reminded me of some of the most important lessons that McKinsey teaches related to giving and receiving feedback.

McKinsey excels at ensuring that all consultants on all projects speak the same language and use the same tools. One of the most important elements is the systematic use of feedback throughout the problem-solving process. I remember learning just how important the language is, especially when you are communicating opportunities for improvement. For example, it is critical that you frame any feedback as being from your own individual perspective. The suggested word choice for sharing feedback is along the lines of: "I have observed that . . .; the effect on me is . . .;" *pause*, "what I suggest is . . ." Receiving feedback is also important, and some suggested tips include listening carefully, asking for examples to ensure understanding and context, and trying not to become defensive (not concluding that I am a "bad" person).

Giving and receiving feedback on the spot is part of the McKinsey culture, and it happens almost daily. More formal feedback is given and received in face-to-face meetings, team learning sessions, and IT-based questionnaires at the end of an engagement. Once again, this is a very structured process and is part of the evaluation of all the senior people within the firm. I once attended a conference featuring a former director from McKinsey; this impressive individual had spent more than 20 years with McKinsey and was one of the firm's top five directors worldwide. When asked how he felt about having moved on from McKinsey, he said he was relieved—he was finally out of the constant spotlight of scrutiny and evaluation. Though feedback can be painful, I'm sure he grew significantly through the process!

STORY FROM THE FIELD—4

Topic: Including the client in organized feedback mechanisms contributes to the engagement's success. Our final story illustrates a fantastic system of coordinating feedback that was developed by one creative ex-McKinsey consultant.

> I worked on developing an electronic feedback system for improving team dynamics. McKinsey consultants are trained to give and receive feedback effectively among themselves, but I found that our clients often are not as comfortable with feedback. We needed another method to share evaluations, particularly in situations where McKinsey consultants and clients have not previously worked together as a team. I worked to create a model that would address this concern, and it has proved to be especially valuable in Asia and other regions where clients are often uncomfortable speaking in a public forum.
>
> In the model, the first step is to address the Talk and Evaluate elements of team projects—to get our clients engaging on and talking about team dynamics. From there, the next step is to collect anonymous feedback, using a Web-based platform. The McKinsey team sends out electronic forms to the client and McKinsey team with normal survey questions (e.g., Are you learning? Do you feel that people are helping you develop?). I have found that this is a good way to break the ice, instead of making people uncomfortable in an open forum. The comments are then aggregated and average statistics are calculated (individual feedback reports are available only to the individual being evaluated).
>
> Typically, these electronic feedback sessions are conducted weekly for the duration of the project. The McKinsey project manager sits down every week to analyze the feedback and

to build statistics. As a rule, the questionnaires bring unsurfaced issues out into the open. This helps us address problems quickly and to further personal and team progress.

The next step of the process is to send our client team's manager the survey results. Note that no senior people (either from McKinsey or from our client) are involved in the process, as that could discourage people from being candid. The project manager then circulates the report within both the McKinsey and client teams. This typically occurs on a Thursday afternoon, and a meeting is held on Friday morning to address the issues that have surfaced. We always make sure to begin each meeting by celebrating accomplishments, and then to discuss opportunities for improvement. Here, the idea is to tease out the issues that were common among many individuals and to come up with satisfactory solutions.

This system has worked very well every time I have implemented it. It has led to exponential improvement in the team's performance, and getting our client to start talking more openly is always helpful. This open communication does take some time to develop, though. The pattern I've noticed is that in the first feedback meeting, few people are willing to talk openly. A few weeks later, clients see the effectiveness of the McKinsey feedback sessions, and slowly start opening up. After three or four weeks, client teams generally seem completely open, and even look forward to these team meetings.

Though my experiences with this model have all been very positive, some teams have had some problems. The feedback sessions occasionally become a platform for criticizing or offending teammates. In some cases, moderators or conflict managers have had to intervene; understandably, our clients in these situations don't like the organized feedback process. The takeaway here is that team members should feel open about discussing team issues, but that these forums must be respectful. It can require coaching and practice to learn how to provide feedback constructively.

STORY FROM THE FIELD—BUSINESS SCHOOL EXAMPLE—1

Topic: Defining clear leaders helps to overcome team conflicts and to improve efficiency. One of our business school stories is from an MBA student at the University of Michigan's Ross School of Business. The respondent describes the common issue of what to do in a peer-based team without any natural leadership roles.

> I was working in a group on a project for Kmart and Citibank. As is common in a top business school, there were problems as a result of clashing personalities and a lack of accountability. With no designated team leader, we had problems at all stages: project definition, organization, delegation, and so on. Thus, we were constantly being pulled in multiple directions. We ultimately recognized this problem and decided to overcome it by implementing a rotating leader position—every two weeks, we named a new leader. After we made this change, our meetings were much more productive; overall, the team was much more successful when we had clearly defined leadership in place.

STORY FROM THE FIELD—BUSINESS SCHOOL EXAMPLE—2

Topic: Role definition and project collaboration balance individual and team responsibilities. Another business school example comes to us from an MBA student at the University of Texas at

Austin. He described a project he encountered while working as a summer associate at a top consulting firm.

> I was working on a team in Chicago for a large company. This was the best team I have ever been a part of, for two reasons.

- *Ownership*. All the members of the team understood what their roles were, and people owned their work chains. This is difficult to find in teams—typically, there are a few really good people who get things done, and there are a few who lag behind. On this team, nobody waited for someone else to tell him or her what to do—each person was proactive in getting things done individually.
- *Collaboration*. Team dynamics were principally collaborative rather than competitive. Whenever anybody seemed to hit a wall, others would try to help. All the team members treated their teammates' problems as their own. One phrase that we used was "making eagles fly together"—the team was full of brilliant people who were very successful individually, but they were also able to work closely and to collaborate to achieve the goals that the team had initially set.

In assigning specific responsibilities, the engagement managers (partners and associate partners) played an active role. They explained all the roles on the project along with the proposed timeline prior to the beginning of the project, and then they sat with each associate on the team and explained what was expected of him or her (these meetings were short and not very detailed). Then, the associates would think through their tasks/assignments individually, devise an approach, and formulate their own work plans. Each associate then shared his or her approach and work plans with the rest of the team so that everybody understood what everybody else was doing throughout the engagement. This was helpful in keeping everybody on the same page—it helped to make sure that there was no overlap or work redundancy, and conversely, it helped to ensure that nothing slipped through the cracks. Additionally, because we understood other team members' roles and problems, we were able to help direct them to people who might be able to provide assistance (e.g., people who had faced similar problems in the past).

CASE STUDY

Put bluntly, there was no chance that we would have finished the project on time without numerous "assists" as described here.

WHAT WE DID

One of the best decisions we made throughout the project was to take advantage of all our resources; specifically, we brought in some other students from the consulting academy (a group within the MBA program) to help us with research. After working on the project for a little while, we realized that there was a ton of research to be done—simply too much research for the five of us. We thought creatively about how we could bring more people onto the project most effectively, and we decided to use an already-existing program to meet our needs.

During "Academy Intensive Week Two," all the students in the consulting academy spend a week of their semester working on a real-life consulting case to gain skills and experience. Because Dr. Friga is the director of the program, he was able to make our Johnson County project the focus of the week (how's that for leveraging your network?). We had an immediate injection of 35 other MBA students to help us with research for the week, which proved to be invaluable. The five of us each led our own group of about five other academy members who helped us to accomplish our own bucket-level goals. Technically, we were called "area experts" instead of team leaders (we didn't want to install any sort of hierarchy), but we all ended up as the natural leaders. After the week, the five of us regrouped and discussed our huge progress, our results, and the implications for the overall project.

Another area in which we really excelled was leveraging expertise. One example that comes to mind immediately is that I was using my legal experience to map out the legal options available to the community to fill its needs, while another team was evaluating the finances. Because these areas were so intertwined, we helped each other with a lot of research and information that was relevant to both teams. We corresponded frequently, both on simple matters (e.g., an estimate of a certain expense) and on complex, high-level matters (e.g., general cost/service trade-offs and prioritization of long-term goals).

WHAT I LEARNED

While working on the Johnson County project, I witnessed how important it is to make use of people's talents, skills, and interests. I believe that when each person is matched with a responsibility that he or she embraces, there are better results for two reasons: first, people with relevant existing knowledge can execute related tasks better than individuals who are approaching a topic cold, and second, when people like what they are doing, they're just better at it. The people who are really at the top of their game are always the people who truly love what they do.

I also learned to be creative in utilizing resources and getting help from others. Most notably, I would have never thought to call in the whole Consulting Academy to help with research, but it proved invaluable. Because of our strict time constraints and the sheer quantity of work we needed to accomplish, we needed all the extra help we could get!

DELIVERABLES

Owner	Work Stream	Data / Research	Findings	Next Steps
Alan	Services	I have been primarily looking at secondary data—statistics about fire, police, water, waste, etc.	My research has been inefficient so far—I feel like I'm spinning my wheels.	I'm meeting this week with a subject-matter expert—hopefully he can point me in the right direction.
Bhavin	Roads	My research has centered on reports, interviews, and observations.	JC roads aren't keeping pace with home values—people in the area expect more.	Now I need to find more statistics and take photos of roads in poor condition.
Rachita	Government / Taxes	I have been comparing the tax rates of unincorporated and incorporated areas and examining the implications.	Incorporation and annexation would both raise taxes, but that would help to finance much—needed improvements.	We need to build a strong case about the benefits that result from increased taxes—the public will be very resistant to tax hikes.
Shalini	Character	Recently, I have focused on determining the effects of the area's rapid growth.	JC's growth is approaching unmanageable rates — this will affect roads, services, schools, etc.	I will examine the results of incorporation and annexation on growth control.
Tim	Incorporation / Annexation	I have been meeting with an expert about city incorporation and analyzing the legal implications of our options.	Our initial hypothesis—annexation—is not the best option.	I'm shifting my research to focus on incorporation as opposed to annexation.

Figure 3-2   Assist: Status Report

4

MOTIVATE

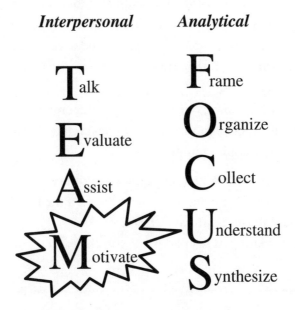

Interpersonal   *Analytical*

Talk Frame

Evaluate Organize

Assist Collect

Motivate Understand

Synthesize

Figure 4-1   TEAM FOCUS Model—Motivate

CONCEPT

Think back to the last team project you worked on. On a scale of 1 to 10, with 1 being completely unmotivated and 10 being the lead cheerleader, how motivated were you? Now assess how motivated your teammates were and also try to identify what motivated them. There were probably varying levels of motivation and sources of motivation on that team—in fact, this is the case for most teams. It is obvious that an unmotivated person (or, even worse, a negatively motivated person) on a team can do significant damage to the team's morale, its interactions, and ultimately its overall performance.

What can we do to increase the motivation and therefore the effort and effectiveness of each team member on a project? The message that is drilled home at McKinsey, and also featured in much research on this topic, is simple to understand but sometimes hard to implement: "Realize that everyone is different and is motivated by different things."

At a very high level, one tends to focus energy on starting with the following types of motivation for consultants on engagements. Do any of these sound familiar?

- Money: hard, cold cash in the form of bonuses or raises
- Promotion: moving to the next level on the totem pole
- Recognition: nonfinancial praise
- Appreciation: a simple thank-you (or two)

RULES OF ENGAGEMENT

Our charge, therefore, is to find a way to deal with the variance in individuals and their underlying sources of motivation.

RULE 1: IDENTIFY UNIQUE MOTIVATORS

The starting point is to find a systematic way to understand people's differences. It is not always easy to get a handle on the underlying factors that drive personality differences in order to strategize about how best to increase idiosyncratic motivation.

Fortunately, behavioral scientists have made a great deal of progress in terms of understanding personality types and predictable behavior. We have come a long way since Maslow's hierarchy of needs (physiological, safety, love/belonging, esteem, and self-actualization). There are several personality profiling tools available these days, and most consulting firms and business schools subscribe to one or more of the following:

- MBTI: Myers-Briggs Type Indicator
- DISC: dominance, influence, steadiness, and compliance
- Big Five: openness, conscientiousness, extraversion, agreeableness, and neuroticism (OCEAN)
- Strengths Finder: "now, discover your strengths"

These are all valuable metrics, and it doesn't matter very much which one you choose—what's more important is what you do with it. At McKinsey, there is widespread use of the MBTI. In fact, when I joined McKinsey in 1996, all consultants were required to take the Myers-Briggs assessment before starting their first engagement. There was also a mandatory team meeting as projects kicked off during which all team members discussed their MBTI profiles, working styles, and personal preferences (along with "pet peeves"). The widespread use of such a tool allows teammates to have a better understanding of where the others on their team are coming from and gives them a clue as to what may motivate them. One caveat to profiling is that a person's default personality can change over time, and there are always mood swings that affect where a particular person is at any one point in time.

For example, here are a few key dimensions of personality types that may surface during the MBTI or other personality profile assessments:

- "Outgoingness"—is the person more extroverted or introverted?

- "Analytics"—is the person more inductive (moving from data to theory) or deductive (moving from theory to data)?
- "Decisiveness"—is the person quick or slow in decision making?
- "Interpersonal interaction"—what is the person's level of sensitivity to team members?

After achieving an understanding of the default personality types, the next strategic move is to determine an appropriate, motivating influence style for successful interaction. Again, rather than try to cover influence styles in great detail (other books do this), I will focus on identifying key influence tactics that relate to team problem solving.

One of the default influence tactics is the authoritarian approach. This involves trying to leverage the authority inherent in a formal title or position in the organization. The truth of the matter is that formal authority goes only so far in terms of motivation (with the possible exception of military organizations during warfare).

To truly inspire someone, the position you hold needs to be backed up by something more. One incremental influence method is the social approach. This style relies on a personal connection with the members of the team. If you establish a friendly relationship, team members may be motivated to do something because they enjoy interacting with you.

Finally, I find that the strongest motivating tool is demonstration. If you would like to inspire a certain behavior (in teammates, classmates, or even family members or spouses), a powerful tool is to demonstrate the desired technique. Somewhat related to this is to remember the Golden Rule, which simply suggests that you do unto others as you would have them do unto you. One of the best examples of this is when you sincerely offer to help someone on her piece of the project and provide some positive energy for her. Not only is such a gesture appreciated for the specific task, but it creates a feeling of goodwill that will almost certainly benefit the team as a whole.

After identifying the personality type of everyone on the team and thinking through interaction strategies, the final step is to develop some unique motivation strategies. One of the best strategies is to focus on the end prize of the entire team's effort. A clear articulation of the benefits to the client or to the organization that you all are part of is quite helpful. A related strategy includes explicit discussions of the personal and professional outcomes each person may realize. For example, these could include recognition, a promotion, or even a financial incentive.

One additional strategy, valuable in all team interactions, incorporates the idea of competition. It does not have to be an intensive competition, with mega prizes to the winners and shame to the losers; it can be just a spirit of comparison with someone else on the team in terms of performance. As an interesting example, one of my good friends happens to own the best steakhouse in Indianapolis (Tom Trotter of the quaint but excellent La Trattoria restaurant in Greenwood, Indiana), and he claims that competition among his servers seems to keep them motivated and on their toes. He shares data related to overall sales, wine sales, and other performance metrics, and then he lets his servers compete in a friendly way. The results are outstanding, and the service is impeccable.

RULE 2: POSITIVELY REINFORCE TEAMMATES

The second Rule of Engagement builds on the discussion in Chapter 3. To my mind, nothing is more motivating than positive feedback for individual accomplishments. Dale Carnegie hit the nail on the head when he observed that the secret to winning friends and influencing people is to focus on them and to share sincere compliments readily. In fact, when I teach this concept to my students, I share a little model developed to guide them through the positive interaction process. Introducing "Paul's Five Ps of Schmoozing":

- *Prepare.* Observe positive actions in the people around you and know their backgrounds.
- *Put others first.* This is a great general paradigm to follow in life.
- *Praise sincerely.* Share your observations, but don't overdo it or seem artificial.
- *Pressure no one.* When interacting, avoid uncomfortable topics and getting too close.
- *Provide value.* In addition to the positive reinforcement you offer, find ways to help the person in the future (one of my favorite tools is to send articles that I think the person will be interested in reading).

It is important that you provide positive reinforcement to team members on a regular basis, especially if they are junior to you in the organization. There must be, however, a limit to the amount of positive feedback you provide. In *The McKinsey Mind*, we refer to this as the "BS Factor"—a point of diminishing returns after the quantity of feedback reaches an indigestible level. People just don't believe that you are sincere in your reinforcement efforts after a certain point. One tip to ensuring sincerity is to focus your feedback on specific observations you make relating to the person's progress toward one of his or her stated developmental objectives for a given project (see Chapter 2).

Occasionally, people say that they have to struggle to find something positive to say about a teammate. I suggest that their framing is off. You can always find something positive to say about any person—it just may take a little more looking. Recently, I spoke at my alma mater, Saint Francis University, as part of an innovative Executive/Professor in Residence Program run by my mentor and friend Dr. Randy Frye, and I addressed this topic as I mentioned how important optimism is for success in teamwork. When a person says that he or she is having a difficult time finding the positive, this may be due to the fact that the person is fixated on one or more negatives and cannot move past them. To achieve the harmony we desire in teams, the key is to find and articulate that positive aspect; once you do so, you will see an immediate increase in motivation—not only in the person you are observing, but in yourself as well.

RULE 3: CELEBRATE ACHIEVEMENTS

The final Rule of Engagement in this chapter is something that McKinsey and most consulting firms still don't develop as fully as they could. The norm for many engagement teams is to have an intense sprint to the end of the project, with team members working their tails off and producing a fantastic deliverable. Exhausted, they may have one last team dinner, and then they move on to their next project. This is a travesty!

The benefits of celebrations are widely known but often forgotten. Good energy knows no bounds and feeds off itself. A celebration is a chance to focus on the positive outcomes of a project, such as client impact, achievement of personal objectives, and joint learning. Holding a postcompletion celebration should be a standard operating procedure. To McKinsey's credit, it is normally very generous in supporting such activities; many times, the celebrations are bigger and better than you might imagine. I remember post-engagement celebrations that included limousines, golf outings, fancy dinners, Arizona retreats, spa treatments, and the like.

My final token of guidance related to celebrations includes the critical success factors for a good postengagement celebration. First and foremost, all team members must be included, from the administrative assistant to the head partner. I have also seen great celebrations that included team members from the client as well. Second, the venue must be a bit different—the standard team dinner just doesn't cut it. If it is a dinner, it must be either at a fun location or very, very fancy. One of my favorite places to take my students during a celebration event is the ESPN Zone, where we can eat, drink, and play all kinds of sporting games. Speaking of games, bowling can also be a fun team-celebration venue—and, of course, you would have to have a friendly competition (as described in an earlier section). The last critical success factor is that, while there can be some discussion of positive observations from the project, the general rule is *no shop talk*! This is a time to bond, to have fun, and to get to know one another in an informal way. There are separate opportunities for reflection and learning from the engagements, but not during the celebration.

My overall point is that you shouldn't underestimate the importance of good, old-fashioned celebrations after current and future engagements. As we get older, many of us start losing this insight!

OPERATING TACTICS

The Operating Tactics for the Motivate element of the TEAM FOCUS model are:

- *Tactic 18:* Identify and discuss one primary and one secondary motivator for each person (the source of energy for that team member).

- *Tactic 19:* Give praise for and celebrate each major team milestone; share compliments with team members on a daily basis.
- *Tactic 20:* Have a social gathering after the project is complete.

STORIES FROM THE FIELD

STORY FROM THE FIELD—1

Topic: Personal responsibility and coaching help to motivate a young associate.   Our first story from the field comes from ex-McKinsey consultant Prof. Dr. Florian Pfeffel, who is currently with accadis Hochschule Bad Homburg in Germany. Florian recalls how important ownership and autonomy are for motivation while on consulting engagements.

> Motivation is a critical component of successful projects. This is especially true for young and new consultants who join your team. I was on a project once at a mobile operator, and after a few weeks of the engagement, the partners and directors weren't happy with the performance of a young associate.
>
> We had different opinions regarding the underlying reasons for the problem . . . some of us thought that his basic capabilities weren't up to par, while others maintained that his underperformance was purely conditional. At the time, he was assigned to supporting various other associates' working packages; he owned nothing himself. We decided to transfer one complete working package to him, and we shifted responsibilities so that the engagement manager was his direct coach.

The effect was excellent—the new associate did an extremely good job on his working package. The reasons for this change were twofold. On the one hand, it was about motivation: the associate could better identify his personal responsibilities, and he was given the flexibility to design and schedule his own plan (in contrast to performing support activities by taking orders). Having his own "baby" turned out to be his major motivating factor, and this probably holds true for most associates.

The second driver of success was the clear coaching assignment. This associate had previously had three different senior associates who were each contributing a little bit to his coaching, and he didn't glean much from the experience. When the EM was assigned directly to the young associate, he was unable to delegate responsibility; the result was that the EM was forced to invest time in assisting and coaching the young colleague. Unsurprisingly, this personal attention quickly paid off, and the associate's performance rose significantly.

STORY FROM THE FIELD—2

Topic: A motivated client and morale-building "quick wins" lead to success.   The second story from the field comes from Pedro Ramos, who has had a wealth of experience: he worked for McKinsey and BCG, moved to private equity, and finally settled with a hedge fund in New York.

I remember two key success factors that were highlighted on a project that was focused on improving the efficiency of a large hospital in London. One key success factor was having very motivated team members, not just on the McKinsey team, but also on the client side. The hospital team was filled with superstars—the hospital's number one and number two doctors were on its team, as was the leading nurse practitioner. These individuals, who exercised power in the hospital, were very excited about the project and very engaged. Hospitals tend to be very political places, with different groups pitting themselves against each other (e.g., doctors, nurses, diagnostics, admin, and so on). To get everybody to agree on anything is very difficult, so it was very helpful to have the top people from multiple groups. It was also very important to give everyone on the project opportunities to shine and to recognize their contributions to the project.

Another key success factor was our strategic decision to focus on "quick wins." The first issues that McKinsey addressed were those that could be easily and quickly solved—the team didn't initially focus on the tasks that could make the biggest impact in the long term, but rather on those that could be implemented in a few weeks. By moving quickly and by having some immediate results, the team was able to quell some cynicism from people outside the project who didn't really believe that consultants could help solve the problem. This, of course, opened the door to pursue bigger, long-term, and high-impact improvement opportunities at the client.

STORY FROM THE FIELD—3

Topic: Understanding personalities and individual drivers helps to motivate both McKinsey and client team members. Our final story from the field comes from Alain Guy, now the vice president of strategy and business development for Convertam in France. He notes that his experiences at McKinsey still greatly affect his work today, and he recalls how important flexibility is in motivating the different members of a team.

> One of the most challenging aspects of working at McKinsey is that in addition to motivating our own consultants, we also have to motivate our clients (who often assign representatives to the engagement team). Many times, and in operational studies in particular, we are placed in a position where we need to motivate our clients to move in a certain direction, and in some cases to undergo significant change. This can be difficult, as we don't have any leverage associated with power or hierarchical influence.

> One of the primary ways we can influence our client is by setting an example; this requires flexibility in dealing with different types of people. McKinsey emphasizes the MBTI (Myers-Briggs Type Indicator) model, with a clear understanding of what influence model should be used with each type of personality. Therefore, a good McKinsey consultant is able to use a unique toolbox for motivating people. I would say that this is not the most well-known aspect of McKinsey, but it is one that is very important.

STORY FROM THE FIELD—BUSINESS SCHOOL EXAMPLE

Topic: Positive reinforcement is key in motivating students who have no enforceable obligations to their organization. We return again to a student from the University of Michigan's Ross School of Business to describe motivation strategies for volunteer teams.

> Because of the voluntary nature of clubs on campus, there are varying levels of motivation. Some people are elected to positions because they feel very strongly about the club and

its objectives, while others only want to spruce up their résumés. I was the president of the consulting club at the University of Michigan, and we had both highly motivated and relatively complacent members on my executive board. What makes things even more difficult is that in this type of club, the members aren't necessarily accountable to anybody—if they shirk their duties, it usually doesn't affect them academically or financially.

In the 2007–2008 year, there were a number of issues that arose because of the motivation discrepancy. Our club was trying to organize a consulting fair, but it was very difficult to get people to perform (especially second-years, who already had jobs). To resolve this issue, we met as a group and discussed the fact that when the current second-years were first-years, they had relied heavily on the second-years to help them get internships; now, as second-years, it is their responsibility to help the first-years.

I introduced the incentive of "board member of the month." It wasn't a monetary reward, but the recognition was motivating to most individuals. I also tried to instill more of a team feeling, where everybody was motivated to help one another rather than just focusing on his or her own tasks. The results have generally been very positive, and I have learned some valuable lessons about how motivation requires different strategies for different people.

CASE STUDY

OK, I have to admit . . . at times, I lost a bit of motivation on the Center Grove Study. But, don't we all at times? Here was how we worked it out.

WHAT WE DID

One of our key motivating factors was our end deadline and deliverable. Being cognizant of our end deadline helped to keep us on track with our work pace and efficiency. All of us got very busy with our full-time school responsibilities. At the same time, knowing that our project would culminate with a presentation to a large group of stakeholders in a public setting motivated us to put in our best efforts. I remember Alan saying once, "It was motivating to know that we were presenting to actual audiences rather than just working on a school project, and to know that at the end of the day we were making a difference. It helped our team maintain perspective when we really focused on the fact that this was going to have a real impact on people's lives."

Despite our own high levels of motivation, we had a tough time motivating our subteams (the consulting academy members that we pulled onto the project to help us with our research during Academy Intensive Week). Because the academy students weren't as personally invested in the project as we were, and because many of them weren't particularly interested in working on a public-sector project, it wasn't a very high priority for many of them. Compounding the problem was that some students had not yet secured internships for the summer, and so they were understandably preoccupied with their search. We all discussed methods of motivating our own groups, and some relevant insights follow.

Alan touched upon the necessity of conveying the big picture to our group members:

> I found that all of us were equally motivated, but it was hard when we all had our own teams and we had to delegate and infuse them with that passion—we understood what the end product was, but they generally didn't. It was hard to motivate

them by just giving them this one silo of information to work with, without putting it into perspective among the large project.

Shalini had a similar approach:

For me, I tried to show them what the impact of their work was going to be, to give them examples from last year. Finally, I helped them with their internship searches. My thought was that if I helped them with their own situations, they would help me with the Johnson County project. My part—character—was hard to get people excited about, so I just assigned people to things they liked.

Shalini made an excellent point by mentioning that if nobody on our subteams stepped up to do the work, we would each end up doing it ourselves. Thus, it was better to try to motivate people and to let people choose what they wanted to work on. We also found that positive reinforcement makes a huge difference. I always make sure to acknowledge people's contributions, especially when someone takes the initiative or puts in some extra effort. I've found that this is far more motivating and increases the team's morale drastically. Similarly, celebrating achievements goes a long way toward keeping people motivated. On the Johnson County project, for example, we celebrated the project's completion by having a very nice dinner with project stakeholders.

WHAT I LEARNED

In this project, I dealt with much more discrepancy in motivation levels than I have in the past—not within our core team, but rather among the additional researchers we pulled in from the consulting academy. I now realize just how difficult it can be to motivate team members when they do not have much buy-in and are not personally invested in the project. Conversely, the driving motivator for our core five-person team was our potential impact on the lives of real people. When trying to motivate myself and others in the future, I will focus on a project's potential impact and also on how individual roles contribute to overall success.

Another one of my key takeaways from this project is the importance of attitude. I have never been more convinced that being upbeat and optimistic is a key component of motivating a team. Everybody likes positive people, and it is fun to work with people who believe in positive reinforcement and frequent celebration!

DELIVERABLES

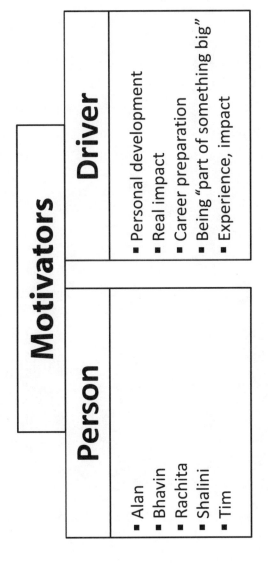

Figure 4-2   Motivate: Motivation Chart

Part 2

FOCUS

5

FRAME

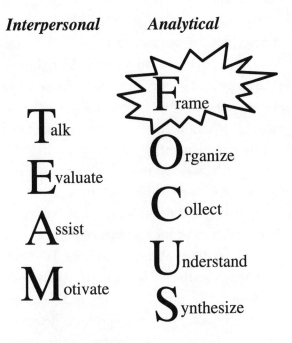

Interpersonal   *Analytical*

Talk
Evaluate
Assist
Motivate

Frame
Organize
Collect
Understand
Synthesize

Figure 5-1   TEAM FOCUS Model—Frame

CONCEPT

Now that you have made it through the interpersonal elements of the model, it is time to move to the analytical elements. Some interviewees describe this portion as the "hard" or "task" portion, as opposed to the "soft" or "people" portion described in Part 1. They may be referring to the context rather than the degree of difficulty (in fact, many people suggest that the "soft" skills are harder to master).

The first element of FOCUS is Frame. In my opinion, supported by the consensus of my interviewees, this is the most important of all the analysis elements. Why? From a system dynamics perspective, framing is especially critical because all subsequent activities are connected to the conclusions reached during this process. If you fail to identify the right question or if you formulate misguided hypotheses, the best-case scenario will be that the team is inefficient, but it eventually gets the right answer. The worst-case scenario is that the team is both inefficient and ineffective, as it arrives at the wrong answer and is slower to get there than would otherwise be the case. You will hear evidence of this in the Stories from the Field later in the chapter.

The origin of the concept presented in this chapter is the scientific method, which has informed scientific and academic inquiry for hundreds of years. Its application to the business world is more recent, having been spearheaded by top strategic consulting firms in the first half of the twentieth century. Increasingly, the use of scientific method concepts such as hypothesis-driven analysis and MECE (mutually exclusive and collectively exhaustive) issue trees is surfacing in corporations and government agencies. These concepts are alive and well in organizations from 3M and Procter & Gamble to the U.S. Navy.

Done correctly, framing is the most important and powerful tool for efficient and effective team problem solving covered in this book. At the same time, it offers the most risk. While I will go into more detail within each of the Rules of Engagement that follow,

I offer the following high-level thoughts for handling the inherent risks of this process:

- Be specific and focused in the development of the issue trees and hypotheses.
- Seek confirming *and* disconfirming evidence to prove or disprove the hypotheses.
- Remember that this is an iterative process and that very rarely do you identify the best answer in your initial thinking.

RULES OF ENGAGEMENT

RULE 1: IDENTIFY THE KEY QUESTION

At first glance, this first Rule of Engagement may appear to be quite simple and obvious, and you may be tempted to move on to the second rule quickly. This is the exact reaction that causes so many problems in the framing process of engagements. Team members are tempted to just get this step out of the way without giving it much thought and move on to the collection of critical data. However, the exact wording of the key question is critical for the analysis portion of an engagement.

Rarely does the first cut at the key question prove to be successful; several iterations are usually required before a team defines the question well. The starting point is the client (or the case in a business school setting) and what it says the problem is. The complication is that the client may sometimes be focusing on a symptom or by-product rather than on the core issue. When I coach students who are trying to land a job in consulting, we spend a lot of time practicing the art of identifying the key question for a particular scenario (the "case interview process"). This is good training, as the ability to identify the key question will be necessary for long-term success in the business world.

So how do we find the key question? The first step is to meet with representatives of the client to understand their perspective and their thoughts on the key question. Remember that the initial attempt to formulate this question may not be exactly right. It is important to make sure that the key question is at the right level of aggregation for the project and the desired outcomes. For example, "How can our organization survive?" is very different from, "How can we improve profitability?" or "How can we generate new business?" The differences lie in scope and specificity—shorter projects must either be more specific or require a lower level of supporting data for their conclusions.

After the initial conversations, the brainstorming process can begin. The starting point, of course, is to list the suggestions from the client and the team members and begin to sort through this list to eliminate redundancy. It is also likely that some of the ideas are subsets of others, so you want to group related ideas.

Shown here is a starting point for key questions in business, but you need to realize that the actual key question will be client- and project-specific. Note also that this is a functional framing—there are other ways to view the key question as well (e.g., level, geography, or time).

- Strategy (based upon a model I created and refer to as the Four Ps of Strategy)
  - What is our *position* in the market (and is it differentiated)?
  - What are our organization's *priorities* (and what should we not do)?
  - What are our organization's *payments* (and are they based on priorities)?

- What is our organization's *performance* (vis-à-vis the competition)?
- Marketing
  - What is our unique selling proposition (and do our customers want it)?
  - How much should we charge for our products?
  - How do we best communicate our offerings?
  - How should we spend our media budget?
- Operations
  - How do we deliver on our business model?
  - How do we reduce manufacturing costs?
  - How do we increase throughput?
  - How do we add capacity?
- Human resources
  - How much do we pay our employees?
  - Do we have the right stuff?
  - How do we increase employee satisfaction?
  - How do we ensure compliance with all regulations?
- Finance
  - How do we value our company?
  - How do we obtain funds for expansion?
  - How are we performing?

Remember, the key question may or may not be functionally driven. It is always contingent upon the nature of the project. A prime example is the case study in this book, which deals with a problem that was not at all related to business functional topics (see the discussion at the end of the chapter).

RULE 2: DEVELOP THE ISSUE TREE

Once the key question has been clearly articulated, the next step is to create an issue tree that will help organize the analysis of options. Since this is covered fairly thoroughly in *The McKinsey*

Mind, I will touch on it only lightly here and focus my energy on discussing ways to implement the ideas on a project. There are essentially two types of issue trees: information trees and decision trees. The starting point is the information tree, which is used to quickly get a sense of the situation under investigation. The decision tree will be elaborated upon in the next Rule of Engagement, "Formulate Hypotheses." The information tree is basically a listing of the key pieces of the current situation. Another way to think of this is that the information tree should summarize, "What is going on?" whereas the decision tree asks, "What can we do?"

An important element of issue tree creation is the concept of MECE. MECE thinking is universally applied at McKinsey and many other top consulting firms. Essentially, MECE is a way of organizing any list in such a way that it has "no gaps and no overlaps." For example, if we were to lay out "buckets" for an investigation related to a profitability project, we would probably draw the issues as shown in Figure 5-2.

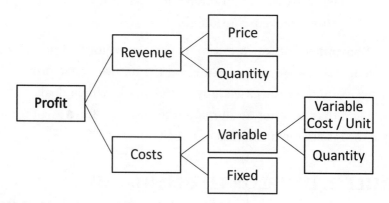

Figure 5-2   Frame: Profitability Issue Tree

An important approach used by McKinsey, other top consulting firms, and business schools involves frameworks. Frameworks are basically issue trees that have been created in the past. Let's face it, your team isn't the first to analyze a profitability issue (or a global expansion, capacity expansion, merger or acquisition, or some other such issue). The first thing a consultant at McKinsey does when assigned a new engagement is to download past reports (which have been cleansed of any confidential information) to see how the problem was framed and investigated in the past. The firm has also developed a set of core issue trees, or thinking on major business issues, that are available to all consultants in written and electronic form. I am not suggesting a "cookie-cutter" approach to problem solving, nor am I implying that the frameworks are actually used as a substitute for analysis. They simply provide a list of topics for consideration, based upon past experiences with similar issues.

One of the by-products of a business school education is the collection of frameworks and methodologies in all the major areas of business problem solving. The professors are subject-matter experts, and one of their jobs is to inform the students of the most important thinking in their area of expertise. This includes providing students with frameworks that summarize key ideas and then teaching them how to use those frameworks. In fact, my research assistants and I have developed a "Killer Slide Deck" of more than 1,000 slides that represents an accumulation of concepts and tools that my students and I have used in the past in all the functional areas of business. The slide deck is helpful for project teams as well as for students preparing for business school case competitions.

Once the MECE issue tree has been constructed, the next step is the prioritization of the issues for investigation. This is a common breakdown point for many teams. The easiest approach is to allocate resources evenly across all the issues in the issue tree (in project management, the resource that is allocated is time and occasionally money). This is a *very bad idea*. The issue tree should be prioritized for analysis based on the key question and the decision criteria that would contribute to maximizing the impact of the ultimate recommendations for the client. Figure 5-3 shows some examples of typical key issues related to some of the more common business scenarios that consultants face. Remember, however, that the actual importance of the specific issue is dependent upon the particular context of the client, team, and environmental considerations.

Revenue Growth	Mergers & Acquisitions
• New products • Add-on services • New markets	• Strategic fit • Synergies • Financial implications

Cost Reduction	Organizational Redesign
• Consolidation • Exit of business lines • Outsourcing	• Structural complexity • Redundancy • Alignment with strategy

Geographic Expansion	New Product Development
• Market size and conditions • Government impact • Resources and capabilities	• Product line mix • Potential market size • Pricing

Figure 5-3 Frame: Business Issues

RULE 3: FORMULATE HYPOTHESES

The final and most exciting part of the Frame element is the development of hypotheses. Hypotheses are potential answers to the key question. The hypothesis becomes the starting point for the decision tree. If the hypothesis is true, what else needs to be true? Since the origin of this approach is the scientific method, we must remember that the hypothesis must be falsifiable; this means that it must be specific and able to be proved or disproved with data. An example of a poor hypothesis would be, "The company should improve its operations"— this is not specific enough to be proven true or false. A better example is, "The company should double its capacity, increase employee annual bonus programs, and cut its product line by 33 percent." Note that there is likely to be more than one ultimate recommendation for any given project (techniques for communicating those recommendations are the subject of Chapter 9). Also, while the hypotheses ultimately become recommendations by the end of the engagement, they are simply hypotheses in the Frame stage, as they are not yet proven.

Intuition is an important consideration in the scientific method. As defined in *The McKinsey Mind*, intuition is essentially gut instinct tempered by experience. It comes into play at several points in the model, including up front (Frame), during the Understand stage, and at the end during the Synthesize stage ("smell tests"). What do you do if you are on a team that is working on a project in an area in which you and your teammates have little or no prior experience and therefore limited intuition? There are several options. One is to parlay experience in a similar or analogous situation in which you have worked. Another is to interview other people who have worked on this type of project and to capitalize on their intuition. A final approach to developing intuition is to create a "basic fact pack" that represents the information the team can gather quickly on the company, industry, environment, competition, and other such areas. The data in the fact pack are not intended to be "pretty" or synthesized—they merely provide some background on the company and some context for its situation that will be helpful in developing hypotheses.

How long should teams spend on the Frame process? I have developed a rule of thumb to answer this question: Approximately 5 percent of an engagement's total time should be spent on framing (assuming that the project time frame is three months or less). So, assuming a three-month project with 360 hours of analysis time, the framing should be finished in about 18 hours or 2 days. In terms of deliverables, this means that the key question has been identified, the issue trees have been drawn out, and the hypotheses have been specified. This ratio can hold true for a 24-hour business school case competition as well, which would mean that the team should complete the framing within 1 to 2 hours. Note again that the process is iterative, and we fully expect adjustments to the initial hypotheses.

My last thoughts on framing are warnings. First, be very careful when communicating hypotheses to clients or others outside the team. I have learned the hard way that if a client believes that you think you can solve a complex business problem in 5 percent of the project time, that client will get nervous. The term *hypothesis* is not generally understood across the board, and it can be interpreted as your proposed answer. It is better to communicate the ideas as potential areas to explore, about which to get the client's input, and ultimately to test with data. One other warning is to remember that this process takes time and you are not expected to nail the solution so quickly. It is helpful to have a direction for testing, but remember to keep an open mind, to seek disconfirming evidence, and *not* to become personally attached to a hypothesis that you proposed!

OPERATING TACTICS

The Operating Tactics for the Frame element of the TEAM FOCUS model are:

- *Tactic 21:* Identify the key question that drives the project, which should be based upon specific discussions with the client.
- *Tactic 22:* Document this question, the scope of the project, and the high-level plan of attack in an engagement letter.
- *Tactic 23:* Specifically identify the temporal (years under study), geographical, and functional areas for the project.
- *Tactic 24:* Avoid the common problem of "scope creep," where additional work is added that is beyond the original parameters of the engagement or is only tangentially relevant to them. Refer back to the base problem, parameters, and engagement letter to mitigate scope creep.
- *Tactic 25:* Develop a general hypothesis that is a potential answer to the problem at hand.
- *Tactic 26:* Develop supporting hypotheses that must be true to support the general hypothesis (for testing).
- *Tactic 27:* Revisit and revise the hypotheses during the project as data are gathered (prove or disprove the hypotheses and if necessary develop new ones).

STORIES FROM THE FIELD

STORY FROM THE FIELD—1
Topic: Framing and prioritizing lead to project efficiency, and a project is finished in less than half of its allotted time. Our first Story from the Field highlights the importance of the Frame

element and the potential efficiency gains in terms of cutting down the number of hours necessary to complete a project. Duncan Orr shares his story from the land down under, based upon his experience with McKinsey in Australia.

> Framing is by far the most important step of the engagement process, in my mind—if this is done right from the outset, the rest of the engagement is usually smooth sailing. Framing avoids unnecessary or irrelevant work (i.e., "boiling the ocean") and ensures that the team is focused solely on the core issues. This means that the client's problem is solved efficiently (something that is particularly important to clients paying McKinsey-size fees!). It also provides team members with a sense of direction and purpose; there is nothing more discouraging for team members than not having a clearly articulated description of the issues they are resolving or, worse, realizing halfway into the engagement that they have been focusing on the wrong set of issues!
>
> This step is not an easy one to perfect. In fact, it can be particularly challenging because the clients themselves often aren't fully aware of the core set of issues. However, having regular client, team, and expert input from the outset will help.
>
> This technique was applied most successfully in a strategy engagement I was involved in where McKinsey was engaged at the last minute to craft a strategy for the client in response to corporate takeover activity it was experiencing. The engagement manager did a great job of defining the set of issues (with help from McKinsey industry experts) and prioritizing only the most relevant "branches" for us to work on (in conjunction with the client). This ultimately led to completing what would normally be a ten-week

engagement in four weeks (with a lot of late nights!). It also led to a standing ovation from the client at the conclusion of our final presentation.

STORY FROM THE FIELD—2

Topic: Several weeks into a project, the project team helps client management define its real key question.   Sisto Merolla, an ex-McKinsey consultant from Italy, describes a common scenario in which a client fails to frame a problem properly, especially in terms of identifying the key question.

> In my experience, framing is the most important part of a project. One of my clients was an electric utility that asked McKinsey to evaluate potential acquisition targets. Some weeks into the engagement, after several interviews with the top managers, we discovered that the real question the company was struggling with was, "Is our generation plants portfolio in line with the future evolution of electricity market prices?"
>
> Once we understood this, we were able to engage the CEO in a very fruitful discussion about what seemed the most likely evolution of the electricity market and what actions could be taken. We came to the joint conclusion that the company did not need to acquire other players immediately, and that the first urgent move was to stop the construction of two new plants. These two additional plants would have imbalanced the generation portfolio, tilting it to an excess of gas-fired plants, which was very dangerous and was not aligned with the corporate strategy.
>
> Sometimes the value that McKinsey adds is helping clients' top managers to take a higher view and understand

the "real" issue instead of rushing into the first solution that comes to mind.

STORY FROM THE FIELD—3

Topic: A client's discomfort with the key question ultimately dissolves the entire engagement.   Our final Story from the Field comes from ex-McKinsey consultant Dr. Florian Pfeffel, who learned how finally getting to the "real" question of an engagement can have a dramatic effect on the ultimate outcome.

Framing is about identifying the key questions of the engagement and ensuring that the approach has the backing of the client's top management. In some cases, the requirement of getting top management buy-in can be a challenging part of the process, especially in public-sector engagements.

I recall an engagement that we conducted that involved a regional cluster development initiative. The mayor of the leading city in this area asked us to support him. Publicly announcing initiatives to support regional businesses is always popular with politicians, and similar activities had had a strong impact in other regions and resulted in a positive media response. However, as in any engagement, acting strategically also implies making unpopular decisions. Politicians often like to focus on the positive results of their initiatives and ignore the negative implications, and this is a problem that we encountered in this engagement.

At the very beginning of the engagement, we recognized that the mayor had started to dilute or postpone required communication activities. Taking a strong stance based upon the implications of the team's finding was not something that the mayor felt comfortable doing. As the purpose of a cluster initiative is to focus on certain relevant industries and, following logically, devote extra attention and subsidies to those industries, there will also be losers who are not part of the focus. The key question of this engagement turned out to be whether the mayor really was willing to lead (i.e., willing to represent, communicate, and act on the probable consequences of the cluster initiative). In this case, he wasn't. We finished the first phase of the engagement and stopped supporting that initiative.

STORY FROM THE FIELD—BUSINESS SCHOOL EXAMPLE

Topic: A lack of information from the client delays the Frame process and decreases project efficiency. Our special Story from the Field comes to us from a student at the Darden School of Business at the University of Virginia. Mike Lewis recalls experiencing a less-than-ideal framing portion of an engagement during his summer internship at BCG. In this case, it was difficult to get the specific framing up front, as the client did not articulate the issues with the needed specificity.

> I was working on a case for a major energy company, and the primary objective of the case was to develop a market size for new products that the company was going to introduce. It sounded clear, but the problem was that there was very poor definition of exactly what the products were going to be. Not knowing precisely how the products were going to be designed made it difficult to look into the consumer research aspect (a task assigned to me). For example, it was hard to know how to do estimates of market share when we had only general ideas—we did not know how the company

was specifically going to design, introduce, and market the product. The situation was ambiguous because there was a key component that was not well defined. When input is poorly defined, the output cannot possibly be well defined.

The basic research was related to crude oil, so the first step was to get names and numbers of producers of crude oil by country and by company. I exerted a huge amount of effort in accomplishing this task, which was not particularly well targeted. I compiled all this information in a database and segmented those producers by size, by geography, and by ownership (many big companies are actually government owned, specifically in Russia, Saudi Arabia, and China). Thus, we were able to get some large-scale, overall market characteristics, but when it came down to what the product was going to be, we were not moving forward very quickly.

We finally learned that product information four weeks into a three-month project, but if the client had been more focused, we could have cut down our time drastically! It is very helpful to have a hypothesis to drive your analysis so that you are moving in a particular direction—even though there is usually a course correction and a shift in focus at some point. In our case, we weren't moving in a specific direction for quite a while.

CASE STUDY

Welcome back. We found that the analytical aspects of the project are just as important as the interpersonal ones. Oh yeah, one other thing—it is tough to get the framing done the first time.

WHAT WE DID

We struggled to identify the key question in this project, drafting revisions on an almost-weekly basis. While this was well past the 5 percent guideline posited by Dr. Friga (we probably landed a decent structure by 10 percent of the project's time). This was due to two factors: first, application of the MECE framework proved troublesome, and, second, the team was uncertain of what exactly the community's objectives were.

We hoped to come up with five different MECE areas so that each of us could own one category; however, identifying appropriate MECE buckets was definitely the most challenging and time-consuming aspect of the Frame component. For example, two of our buckets were legal issues and financial issues, which we thought would be relatively independent of each other. However, after we started researching, we realized that they were tied together in many ways. For example, the legal form of incorporation affects financing as well as the negotiating stances of the parties who would be partially responsible for determining the financing. Because of this type of redundancy, we continually revisited our bucket issues and produced many iterations—the categories we ultimately ended up with were very different from those we initially devised.

A lot of our difficulty with bucketing was related to scope creep: the more we thought and researched, the more difficult it became for us to define our parameters. For example, the seemingly straightforward category of "services" ended up requiring a specific definition, complete with a list of what does and what does not fall under its umbrella.

Complicating matters, the buckets we settled on were not necessarily equal in terms of workload. Alan observed:

> Halfway through the semester, we realized that some people were going to have much more work than others,

determined by the bucket they were leading. For example, with police and fire, we were constantly reevaluating our approach to analysis as well as appropriate metrics (e.g., crime prevention vs. punishment). All of this reworking ended up being very, very time consuming.

Because we were finally happy with our buckets, because we wanted to preserve simplicity, and because we needed to keep responsibilities clearly defined, we decided not to rearrange our buckets or to have team members jump onto other members' topics. Instead, we tried to fix the disparity in required time commitments by allocating nonbucket responsibilities in a way that would make overall workloads more balanced.

As I mentioned, the second issue that made framing the problem difficult was being unsure of what the community wanted. Because of the nature of our project (presenting to a large group of extremely emotionally invested stakeholders in a town meeting), taking the audience into consideration was necessary. Under the guidance of Dr. Friga, we tried to structure our research, our deliverables, and especially our presentation to address the needs of the audience. Alan shared his thoughts about audience awareness:

> While framing, it was important that we consider who the audience was and what it wanted to hear; the members of our audience wanted to know what their situation was, what their options were, and what they should do. As we expected, the audience reacted negatively to the inevitable consequence of our recommendation to incorporate—increased taxes.

Because the audience members were so personally affected by the situations outlined in our project—and would be drastically affected by our recommendation, if it were enacted—we had to be very careful in our wording. For some issues (such as improved roads), we presented as if ours was a receptive audience, whereas for others (like increased taxes), our presentation techniques were adapted to fit the demands of a hostile audience.

Interestingly, we ultimately disproved our original hypothesis. At the beginning of the project, we thought that the area of Center Grove should be annexed by Bargersville. Because we subscribed to a hypothesis-driven approach, we started collecting data in an attempt to support our original proposition. However, we soon realized that the data (or at least our assumptions about potential citizens' reactions to such a merger) actually disproved our hypothesis, and we concluded that Center Grove should incorporate as a new city (this would deal with annexation resistance).

WHAT I LEARNED

The most important time we spent throughout the project was the initial period of brainstorming, framing the problem, and debating potential MECE buckets. This took longer than we expected, but it was well worth it in the end. Knowing exactly what we were looking for while researching and understanding where the project was going as a whole helped us to home in on the important issues and to avoid extraneous, unproductive work.

Although persistence and dedication are great qualities, it is important that you be flexible enough to change your mind when research does not support your initial hypothesis. I was impressed with this team's ability to consider data objectively and to amend our research and recommendations accordingly. A key reason we were able to do this is that we kept our eyes open throughout the project—defining our framing and bucketing approach was really an ongoing process, and we were constantly reexamining our underlying assumptions.

DELIVERABLES

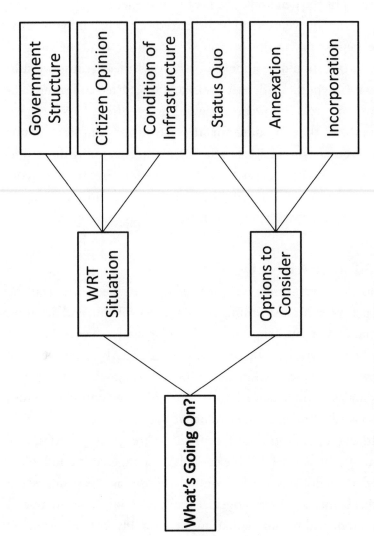

Figure 5-4 Frame: Information Tree

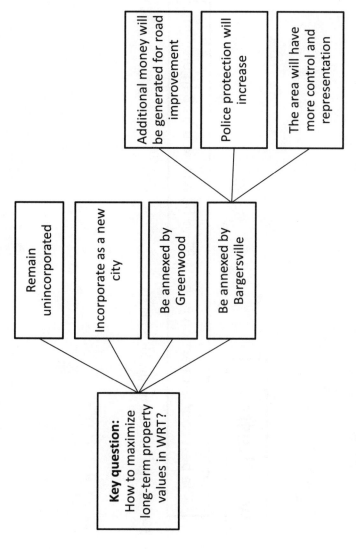

Figure 5-5 Frame: Decision Tree

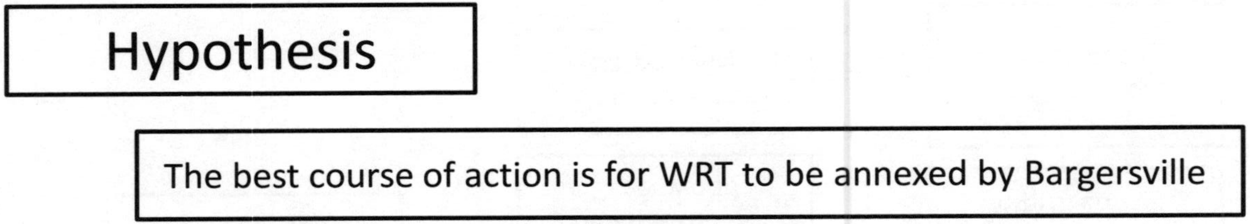

Hypothesis

The best course of action is for WRT to be annexed by Bargersville

Figure 5-6   Frame: Articulate the Hypothesis

6

ORGANIZE

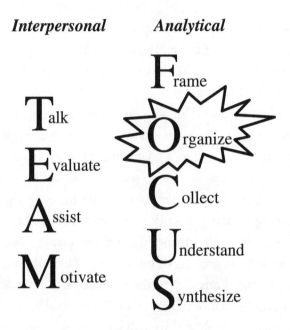

Interpersonal   *Analytical*

Figure 6-1   TEAM FOCUS Model—Organize

CONCEPT

Once the problem is framed properly, we need to organize our analysis efforts in a very strategic manner. Remember that our primary goal in this process is both increased effectiveness (doing the right thing) and increased efficiency (doing it well). The underlying assumption here is that many team problem-solving adventures could be improved. What are the typical issues associated with nonstrategic approaches to team problem solving?

I have generally found that there are three primary issues with the Organize bucket of analysis. All of these issues stem from problems that probably arise because of poor framing (see the system dynamics discussion in the previous chapter). The first issue occurs when a team organizes around the wrong things. Essentially, the issue tree either is not done in an MECE way or, more commonly, is not properly prioritized. The next issue is related, and it has to do with the allocation of resources in the team problem-solving process. The easiest (but not the most efficient) way to assign people to tasks is just to split things up evenly, without giving much thought to the workload and/or the impact of each area on the eventual end product.

The final mistake that teams typically make in the Organize phase is failing to design a work plan that is centered on testing the hypotheses developed during the Frame phase. The scientific method requires the proving or disproving of hypotheses, which are essentially potential answers to the key question. Spending a lot of time and energy gathering data on a more general basis (i.e., gather as much data as possible and we will see what we find—inductively) may be helpful in some circumstances (e.g., when you have absolutely no previous experience in this area), but it generally leads to gathering and analyzing irrelevant data, which is inefficient.

RULES OF ENGAGEMENT

Every team organizes in some fashion or other. The key differentiator is how strategically the team is organized. I have been part of many teams that have spent very little time thinking about the work streams because they wanted to get to what they saw as the real value-adding work quickly—data collection. The truth is that the organization is the value-adding work, and top consulting firms like McKinsey give careful thought to the problem-solving approach. Many consultants refer to this process as developing a "work plan," and I break that "work plan" concept down into two separate components, as described in the first two Rules of Engagement (process map and content map). The final rule pertains to the all-important "story line" that serves to guide the entire process.

RULE 1: DEVELOP A HIGH-LEVEL PROCESS MAP

The first step in organization is to create a *process map* (this is my terminology, and it is my understanding that consultants at McKinsey may not use this exact nomenclature; still, they always create a process map, whether they call it that or not). The process map does not need to be complex or extremely specific. In fact, I was a bit surprised by the level of formality of the initial process maps at McKinsey. While working in the turnaround and bankruptcy practice at PricewaterhouseCoopers, we created meticulous process maps, partially because we were part of an accounting firm and partially because we had to report our time charges in six-minute increments. The truth of the matter is, the process map for a typical consulting project should be straightforward and should answer only a few key questions:

- What needs to be done at a high level?
- Who will do what?
- What will the end result look like?
- When will it be done?

Of course, during a project, there will be some adjustments made in the schedule, and the process map may need some updating. If the process map is kept simple, such updates will not require an onerous effort. Of course, if you are working on a longer project or one that involves more team members, the complexity of the process map increases. However, my tip is not to put too much specificity in the process map or to start combining it with the content map, which is described next.

RULE 2: CREATE A CONTENT MAP TO TEST HYPOTHESES

The content map is the element of the organization process that can have the most impact on the efficiency of a project. It is here that the team determines its analytical priorities and its approach for testing hypotheses. Again, while McKinsey consultants will not necessarily use the term *content map*, I find it to be helpful when teaching the organization component to other consultants, executives, and students.

The content map is very engagement-specific. It is an outgrowth of the framing process discussed in the previous chapter. Once the team determines the key question, outlines the issue trees (information and decision), and creates one or more hypotheses, the testing must begin. An efficient team will focus its energy on identifying and testing the most important subhypotheses that must be true if the overall hypothesis is to be true. You can test any number of statements that may seem related to the hypothesis, but what must you really know to determine if the hypothesis is valid?

The challenge, of course, is related to the determination of those supporting thoughts or subhypotheses. For Z to be true, X and Y must also be true, and how are we going to prove the truth of X and Y? Because this process is so context-specific, it is impossible to tell you, a priori, what the subhypotheses should be. When I teach this material, I offer the following advice:

- Use frameworks from business school and from textbooks to generate ideas.
- Examine past projects that had some similarity to this project (e.g., from the same industry, the same function, the same business issue, and so on) to see what has been used in the past.
- Create a diverse team to participate actively in the brainstorming process (see Chapters 1 through 4 for more advice related to this process).

RULE 3: DESIGN THE STORY LINE

The final Rule of Engagement in this chapter relates to a critical organizing element for consulting projects: the story line. I cannot tell you how many times I heard the question, "What's the story?" in the halls of McKinsey. The story line is essentially the outline for the final presentation at the end of the project. This is one of the secrets of efficient problem solving: you begin working on the final presentation story very early in the project—almost on day one. Right after the framing is finished and before systematic data gathering commences, the team should develop an initial story, brainstorming about both the actual story line and how to deliver it.

What happens if the story changes? It will! Count on it. One of the core consulting skills is flexibility and the ability to adapt. As the team tests the hypotheses with data, some hypotheses will be proven false; in fact, in the end, the entire story may be very different from the original version (we experienced that to a certain degree in our case study). This is normal and to be expected. The real risk in this whole process is if there is no flexibility and people become personally attached to their initial hypotheses, focusing simply on proving them without considering disconfirming evidence.

The story line migrates into a "storyboard" as data are collected and key insights are developed. One way to think of this is that the story line is the ongoing outline; it can perhaps be best portrayed on a portrait document with supporting pyramids (this concept will be elaborated upon in Chapter 9). The storyboard, then, is the translation of the story into a landscape slide deck, with insights at the top and data in the middle (also discussed more thoroughly in later chapters).

All three of these Rules of Engagement are illustrated in the deliverables for the case study at the end of the chapter. The exact format and obviously the ingredients of the maps will be different for your project, but these examples may serve as a helpful template as you move forward.

OPERATING TACTICS

The Operating Tactics for the Organize element of the TEAM FOCUS model are:

- *Tactic 28:* Maintain objectivity as the hypotheses are tested during the project.
- *Tactic 29:* Use frameworks as a starting point to identify issues for analysis.
- *Tactic 30:* Explicitly list the types of analysis and related data that the team will and will not pursue (at least at that stage in the project life cycle).
- *Tactic 31:* Revisit this list if the hypotheses are modified.

STORIES FROM THE FIELD

STORY FROM THE FIELD—1

Topic: Taking the time to make an educated hypothesis leads to project efficiency. Our first Story from the Field comes from an ex-McKinsey consultant who highlights how important it is to have the right hypotheses to ensure efficient analysis.

> There is an important caveat to the McKinsey problem-solving approach. Consultants are pushed from day one to engage in hypothesis-driven problem solving. I was once asked to be involved in a team that was struggling. The engagement was nominally an effort to improve the organization of an oil and gas company. The team had already conducted two or three team problem-solving sessions, including pulling in organization experts, and generated lots of hypotheses to test. This effort was not leading the team to any ideas or insights into how the company's organization needed to change to make the company more effective. The team and the client were becoming a bit frustrated.
>
> When I met with the team, the first question we discussed was, "How does this oil company make money?" The short answer was that no one knew. Two days of work later, we had a good handle on the company's sources of value creation. We used this material to focus another hypothesis-generation meeting on the company's possible organization issues. This meeting yielded a very robust set of hypotheses, and the study proceeded very smoothly from that point forward. My big "ah-ha" from this experience is that hypothesis-driven problem solving is a great approach, but you have to have gathered enough basic facts beforehand to inform the effort, or else you can end up wasting lots of time.

STORY FROM THE FIELD—2

Topic: Failure to implement well-framed, hypothesis-driven approaches leads to extraneous work and inefficiency. Fred Humiston, who is currently with Celgard, recalls two McKinsey projects where the issue tree development process certainly had room for improvement.

On two of my projects, we learned some valuable lessons about the importance of getting the issue tree right in the initial stages of the project. I had been trained in solving problems in a rigorous way (McKinsey's key to success), but sometimes we failed to rigorously adhere to our problem-solving method, or we abandoned it altogether. As a result, certain critical issues remained unresolved, and both our efficiency and effectiveness suffered. The first project where this was important was one involving a financial institution that asked the firm to help it get into a line of business that was considered standard for such organizations. In fact, the financial institution had been in this line of business before, but had sold it and was now looking at reestablishing it. The key questions were, "Should the financial institution enter this line of business again, and, if so, how?"

We established the issue tree (decision tree) with two high-level buckets, "do it yourself" vs. "partner with somebody," but the tree soon began to break down. We struggled with the next level of the issue tree—for "go it alone" we looked at the client's internal capabilities and constructed a financial model, whereas for the partnership situation we examined the pros and cons of each potential partner. This really wasn't an apples-to-apples comparison between the two options, but the team leadership decided not to come up with any clearer method to compare them. Two months later, we had evaluated the two options completely on their own, but without any meaningful comparison. Ultimately, we came up with a very simple answer, which was that any financial institution of this size should be able to profitably operate the line of business that we were investigating, and if they could do it on their own there was no point in partnering. However, only a limited portion of our work, and certainly not much problem solving, actually contributed to reaching this conclusion. To be honest, we could have saved the client money and time and had a better experience if we had focused more on framing before diving in.

The other project illustrated how important it is in working with a client to have that client understand the value of a clear problem-solving approach. This engagement involved a huge retail client that was deciding whether and where to expand overseas (not an uncommon project for McKinsey). Since it was only my second engagement, I was reluctant to question the problem-solving approach or the reaction to client input. We decided not to use a hypothesis-based method because the client didn't want us to have preconceived notions—it told us to look at the whole world and boil down the results. I sensed that something was amiss, and, looking back, I guess this should have been a red flag. However, this was a big client, so we wanted to please it and didn't push back. While we had a sense that we should be framing this in a strategic and financial issue tree, we spent six months doing a lot of work that was of almost no use to the client at all. We spent endless hours analyzing companies and country portfolios that only tangentially related to the key question, "Should the company expand internationally?" It could have been a golden moment for McKinsey's strategic acumen to shine through, an opportunity to define what a major player wanted to be in the world, but in the end the quality of our work was, in my view, below the traditional McKinsey standard. Oddly enough, the client was pleased with the work, but there was a palpable sense of let-down throughout the McKinsey team.

STORY FROM THE FIELD—3

Topic: Clear organization drives the success of one project, while failure to align team members toward a single goal contributes to mediocre results in another.   Mario Pellizzari, who spent four years in the McKinsey office in Milan and is now with Egon Zehnder International, describes some pluses and minuses of organizing around hypotheses.

My first example is related to a business plan for one of the largest Italian companies, in which the McKinsey team was involved in many different parallel work streams for the client. Realizing how important it was for all of the teams to be working on high-impact areas, I was constantly involved with the coordination and prioritization efforts among the teams.

In fact, we developed an overarching model that described the key questions, hypotheses, and potential recommendations in each of the areas while synthesizing the impact and coordinating synergistic knowledge creation. One director exerted considerable effort, leading the engagement managers to maintain their focus and organization of teamwork. Such an approach of central alignment, framing, and organizing was extremely helpful, even if it seems simple to do.

My second story was not as positive. The success of any engagement is determined by how clearly a proposal is defined at the outset of the project. The agreement with the client should be very clear in terms of the following: the result, what the engagement will achieve, the involvement of the client, and how to align both the team and the client. Based on my experience, this agreement is well defined in about 99 percent of engagements, but occasionally one slips through the cracks.

In a merger project I worked on, two separate partners were not on the same page during the organization effort. The two McKinsey teams went down different paths, did not coordinate, and at times seemed to be producing contradictory results. Much of the problem stemmed from the facts that one team did the work plans for both teams and that the players on the project teams never really aligned their goals. In the end, I believe it turned out to be one of those rare cases where our efforts did not translate to significant added value for the client.

STORY FROM THE FIELD—BUSINESS SCHOOL EXAMPLE—1

Topic: Division of responsibilities to avoid redundant efforts and frequent communication lead to an efficient and thorough engagement. Ben Kennedy of the Fuqua School of Business at Duke University describes some takeaways after working as a summer associate at a top strategy-consulting firm.

I learned quite a bit during my internship. My project involved creating a short-term growth strategy for a private equity firm's client that was hoping to go public. One complication was that the company served a number of different industries, each with a different growth trajectory.

The project was organized around three different work streams, each with a different manager. I worked on several aspects of the project and found it quite motivating, as I was able to see how the pieces fit together. I generated insights as I analyzed the data, and I found that the insights became more and more developed as others in the different streams looked at the results. I learned the power of checking in with the team on a regular basis, as well as just how helpful a nice conference table and whiteboard can be.

When it came to organizing our data collection, we were very careful about splitting up the collection/generation effort—it just doesn't make sense to have everyone looking at the same raw data, articles, databases, spreadsheets, and other such material, because it is so inefficient.

One other takeaway for me was related to gathering information from the client. You want to get as much first-hand information as possible, but you also have to separate fact from opinion. You have to seek out the true experts in the firm and realize that some folks have particular agendas that explain why they tell you things (e.g., concern about losing one's job). I found it helpful to put in process steps by which I could verify what I heard through data and interviews with people at different levels within the company.

STORY FROM THE FIELD—BUSINESS SCHOOL EXAMPLE—2

Topic: Definition of team goals and awareness of others' progress help a busy team win a case competition.   Our last Story from the Field comes from Juan Pulido, an MBA student at the Darden School of Business at the University of Virginia. Juan describes three critical success factors that helped his team win a major business school case competition.

The first step was to get everyone on the same page. Our team had a high level of focus, and we were all very enthusiastic. We had the same goals and guiding principles: "learn, have fun, and aim for first prize." In terms of organization, the first step was to have all five group members brainstorm about how to approach the project and what they thought the end result should include. We then narrowed the list and drew a tentative storyboard to help us Frame our research and define its scope. From this storyboard, we were able to incorporate hypothesis-driven analysis; by thinking backward, we were able to discern what intermediate steps were necessary to achieve our desired end result.

Our division of work and assignment of roles were democratic and informal, as each person volunteered to own a particular work stream based on past experience or interest. We then made a Gantt chart that included due dates and intermediate goals (though this sounds professional, it was a relatively informal process). This helped to keep everybody on the same page and aware of what the other team members were doing.

The case was four to five days long, and because it took place in the middle of interview season, everybody was extremely busy, and the situation was hectic. There were definitely some conflicts during the project, but through daily, open communication, we were able to avoid major misunderstandings and confrontations. Frequent communication was necessary to keep everybody on the same page and on task, as our schedules didn't always allow for lengthy team meetings.

There was no clear leader in this group, which was randomly chosen (we all sat next to each other in class). But by working carefully together and organizing strategically, we were able to achieve our goal and win first prize!

CASE STUDY

Not a whole lot of issues here. Dr. Friga and Chris Cannon played an active role in organizing our efforts. We also benefited from all of our hard framing work as described in the previous chapter.

WHAT WE DID

We had spent a great deal of time and energy framing the problem and defining and assigning MECE buckets, with the result that the project's organization really fell into place quite easily. In the initial stages of the project, we focused on creating a high-level process map that served to guide us throughout our research. We revised this map as our research closed off some avenues and opened up some others. This helped us to focus on important areas and not to boil the ocean.

As the project developed, we shifted our focus increasingly to the story, with our key question serving as the starting point. We knew that we could have all the data in the world and very convincing arguments, but if we didn't have a coherent story that was easily followed, our presentation would be ineffective. In order to have the most powerful presentation, Shalini and Rachita spent a long time putting all our slides together and organizing them into a logical sequence. Afterward, Dr. Friga and Chris Cannon edited the deck, rearranging and tweaking the slides so that our story would build and finish with force.

WHAT I LEARNED

At the end of the day, the story is what matters. A lot of work needs to be done behind the scenes in order to craft the story well, but ultimately the most important thing is to come up with a story that the audience can follow and that produces the desired impact/effect. You can have great ideas and great research to back it up, but if you don't present the story well, it falls flat. We found that by thinking about the story earlier in the process, especially during the Organize phase, our work was both more effective and efficient. Many times we were tempted to gather data or do some analysis on areas or topics that ultimately were not that important. This becomes clear as you consider where it would fit in terms of the ultimate story and especially in terms of the final presentation.

DELIVERABLES

Phase	1	2	3
Primary Objective	**Frame, Organize, and Collect** ▪ Develop a situational understanding	**Understand** ▪ Create a preliminary story line	**Synthesize** ▪ Finalize report
Deliverables	▪ Work plan ▪ Preliminary fact pack ▪ Interview summaries ▪ Incorporation example overview (Avon)	▪ Ghost deck ▪ Interview summaries ▪ Revised fact pack	▪ Executive summary ▪ Final report ▪ Appendix
Completion Date	February 19	March 13	April 16

Figure 6-2   Organize: Process Map

Major Area	Subarea	Who	Key Tasks	Due Date
Services Comparison	Fire	Alan	Meet with the fire department—discuss options and concerns	Feb. 19
	Police	Alan	Meet with the police department—discuss options and concerns	Feb. 19
	Water	Alan	Research the impact of population growth on water requirements	Mar. 13
	Waste	Alan	Research the impact of population growth on waste removal services	Mar. 13
	Roads	Bhavin	Quantify the problem—how many miles of bad roads are there in the unincorporated area? WRT?	Mar. 5
Control Considerations	Zoning	Shalini	Find current zoning policies/laws—business friendly?	Feb. 26
	Character	Shalini	Meet with citizens to discuss their area's unique character and how to preserve it	Mar. 5
	Economic development	Tim	Research business growth in unincorporated areas—compare with incorporated areas	Feb. 26
	Ordinances/laws	Tim	Research laws—how do you actually incorporate?	Mar. 13
	Green space	Shalini	Research amount of green space in the unincorporated area vs. Greenwood and Bargersville	Mar. 5
Resource Requirements	Financial	Rachita	Research the costs of incorporation	Mar. 13
	Organizational	Rachita	Find out what organizations/people will be involved	Feb. 26
	Legal	Tim	Meet with Alan Yackey—discuss Avon case	Feb. 19

Figure 6-3   Organize: Content Map

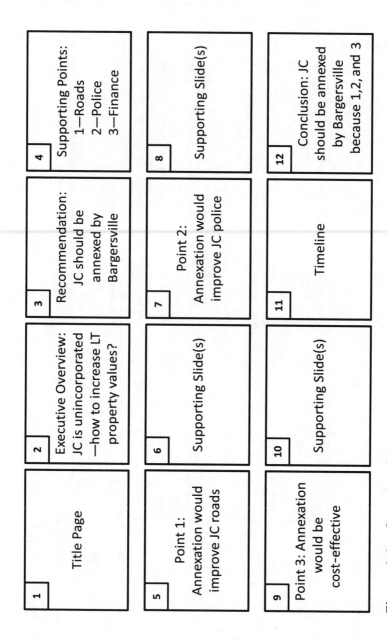

Figure 6-4 Organize: Story Line

7

COLLECT

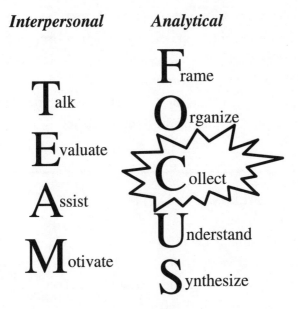

Figure 7-1   TEAM FOCUS Model—Collect

CONCEPT

This is the shortest chapter in the book, and also the most straight-forward. Though collecting data is mundane, it is still an important element of the team problem-solving process. Why are data important? First and foremost, data are the tools that are used to prove or disprove the hypotheses developed during the analytical process. They enable the problem solvers to arrive at conclusions that are (hopefully) correct, and therefore effective. Finally, the data become the basis for reports and presentations when the final recommendations are presented (this will be covered much more thoroughly in Chapter 9).

So what is the key challenge in the data-collection process? The most common problem may be too much information. Given the outstanding search tools, electronic databases, and codified knowledge that are available, teams generally collect more information than they use; as a result, they are inefficient in terms of finding the important information for the issues at hand.

RULES OF ENGAGEMENT

The Rules of Engagement given here all focus on increasing efficiency and effectiveness during the data-gathering process, with a primary goal of weeding out excess information.

RULE 1: DESIGN "GHOST CHARTS" TO EXHIBIT NECESSARY DATA

This Rule of Engagement may have caught your attention because it includes what may be a new concept for your teams. When I teach the TEAM FOCUS model, this is one of the most challenging tools to introduce to teams, especially if they are not accustomed to working with draft deliverables.

What is a ghost chart (some refer to this as a "ghost slide," although the terms are used interchangeably herein)? It is basically a draft slide that is used to capture ideas at an early stage in the problem-solving process. It comprises a title (usually at the top of the slide), a data label, and the data (or a sketch of what the data will be once collected). The most important part of the ghost slide, and the only part that should reflect any substantial amount of "analytical energy," is the title of the slide. The title is in sentence format, and it states the insight—the "so what"—of the slide. An example of a title would be, "The revenue from widget sales is on a steady decline." The title is a specific identification of the anticipated data that will be shown on the slide. At this stage in the process, remember, we are not exactly sure of what the data will be, so the label is an educated guess as to what we expect to find to test our hypotheses. An example of a graph label would be "Widget Revenue 2003–2008."

I find that many times, teams will create the label and wait until the data are gathered to take a stab at the title. It is important to be thinking in terms of insights related to the story all the way through the process, not just at the end! Recognize that the slide title and even the data label will probably change over the course of the project, and that there is nothing wrong with that—in fact, it is expected!

The final part of a ghost chart is a sketch of the data. Do not take the time to format a sophisticated chart with representative data, in other words, the data you expect to gather. All that is necessary is a very rough sketch, by hand at first, and then with a template chart that represents how the data may be displayed. Basic chart formats taught at McKinsey (and in most consulting firms) are listed here and are also becoming standard fare in Microsoft PowerPoint. Note that we will cover this much more thoroughly in Chapter 9.

- Bar charts (vertical or horizontal)
- Pie charts (components)

- Waterfall charts (composition, building to a total)
- Era charts (from–to)
- Flowcharts (steps)
- Gantt charts (activities and timeline)

The biggest problem consultants have with creating ghost charts is their reluctance to document their ideas without thorough data collection and analysis. This was a struggle for me early in my career. However, it is important to realize that the problem-solving process is iterative and evolves over time. The formal creation of draft deliverables is a great way to make the process more efficient. This had been especially apparent to me when working with MBA students in team projects or case competitions. Rather than "wasting" time creating ghost charts, the teams just gather data and analyze them, and they continue to gather and analyze until the very end of the process, when they finalize the story and create charts. One problem with this approach is that the data are not as convincing as they might be when displayed in chart format; additionally, at the end of the project, these teams often find that they are missing key data related to their story. These problems can be eliminated by crafting and reviewing ghost charts throughout the process. Throughout the halls of McKinsey, there used to be an expression, "Create a chart a day," which highlighted how important it is to document your observations and insights in the form of a powerful chart that you share with your team. In reality, though, you will probably need to create many charts per day.

RULE 2: CONDUCT MEANINGFUL INTERVIEWS

Interviews are a critical part of the data-collection process. In most consulting projects, interviews have more impact on the problem-solving effort than the secondary data. Why? First and foremost, the interviewees can provide direct and interactive feedback about the hypotheses you are testing. Many times, especially if you are interviewing client personnel or subject-matter experts, your interviewee can provide original thoughts related to past experiences, issues, and potential outcomes. One of my main research interests is knowledge management, and I have found that the vast majority of knowledge is stored in people's heads, not codified in documents (despite the huge investments companies continue to make in codifying such knowledge). Interviewees can also save you time in your search for secondary data, as they are often able to direct you to the most valuable codified knowledge in their field. This is particularly valuable when your team has limited familiarity with the topic under study. So, make sure that strategic interviews are a key part of your data-collection effort.

When it comes to the interview itself, one of the most common problems is that the interview is poorly conducted, and as a result is ineffective. The following three tips can help ensure that your team conducts meaningful interviews:

- *Before the interview.* The quality of the interview is likely to be determined well before the interview even takes place. The two key steps are (1) identify the right people to interview (who has unique knowledge about this topic, who can respond to the hypotheses, and who will be involved with implementation or subsequent efforts?) and (2) develop and share an interview guide (what are the three key topics to cover?).
- *During the interview.* A common mistake in interviews is to get carried away with trying to gather as much information as possible. A better strategy is to spend the time very carefully—for example, on insights and reactions to a hypothesis—and to build a positive relationship that would allow for comfortable follow-up conversations.

- *After the interview.* While a "thank-you" e-mail, letter, or
  card is certainly a good idea, the real recommendation
  I have for you is to document, document, and document.
  Within 24 hours, the consultant must document the key
  takeaways from the interview, including quotes and
  references to additional material. Also, share your
  interview notes with the other members of your team
  to keep them in the loop on your research. McKinsey
  utilizes a template form and provides training in interview
  notes documentation.

RULE 3: GATHER RELEVANT SECONDARY DATA

Gathering the most relevant and powerful data is the backbone of
good consulting and the opportunity for junior consultants or
business school students to shine. Remember, since our goal is to
be as efficient and effective as possible, we have to address
ways to minimize the gathering of data that are not important to
our story.

The starting point in strategic data gathering is to keep the
context of the key question and the hypotheses in mind as you gather
the data. If you start gathering a ton of data before you have really
fleshed out your issue tree and internalized the key question, you
will ultimately gather information that is perhaps only tangentially
related to the core analysis. Have you ever worked on a project
where the team gathered extra data and created charts that were
not used in the final deck or even the supporting appendix? If you
continue to ask the relevant questions as you gather data, you will
be more efficient. This topic will be covered more thoroughly in
the next chapter, but teams must question the potential impact of
the data during the collection process as well.

Of course, the foundation of good data collection is familiarity with electronic resource tools, especially for consultants working in smaller firms or business school students. The largest consulting firms of the world, such as McKinsey, employ research specialists who assist with and often run the data-gathering process. For the rest of us, electronic databases and search tools can be our best friends or our worst enemies. The only way to learn how to make them your best friends is to get to know them and spend a lot of time with them. Most of the top business schools have access to the best data-gathering databases in the world—and you will be astounded at the amount of information that is available to you with only a few keystrokes.

When I work with students (and executives), I start by having them do an inventory of the tools available to them in their school or company. For example, some of my favorite research databases for typical business problems include the following (note that these sources are always in flux):

- Factiva—a great starting point
- Market Research Monitor—short industry reports and market sizing
- InvestText Plus—in-depth industry reports by investment banks and others
- Mergent Online—deep data on firms (can download financials)
- Reuters Business Insight—specific industry reports
- MarketLine—quick hits on companies and industries
- S&P NetAdvantage—well-regarded industry data
- Frost & Sullivan—international industry data
- Hoover's—company data on the big firms
- Periodicals and newspapers—current news (e.g., *Business-Week*, the *Wall Street Journal*, and so on)

- Nielsen—market metrics
- Google—the catch-all

Just as with any tool, the only way to become proficient is to practice. I recommend that you force yourself to try all of these tools (and others) at least once to get a sense of what they can do for you. Ultimately, you will find your favorites and learn how to navigate them extremely well. Google continues to advance its offerings in this space every day and even offers sites for searching for data, sharing documents, and working live on team projects.

My last suggestion is brief but critical: *always document the source of your data on your charts*. This is important for credibility (the idea is sufficiently supported), authenticity (it was not made up), and traceability (we can go back to the original source at a future point).

OPERATING TACTICS

The Operating Tactics for the Collect element of the TEAM FOCUS model are:

- *Tactic 32:* Design ghost charts to exhibit the necessary data that are relevant to the overall story.
- *Tactic 33:* Use primary research, and especially interview the client personnel; document interview guides ahead of time, and share the insights with the team in written form within 24 hours.
- *Tactic 34:* Always cite the source of the data on each chart created.

STORIES FROM THE FIELD

STORY FROM THE FIELD—1

Topic: Strategic data collection that includes heavy use of ghost charts makes all the difference. Our first data-gathering story from the field is a classic tale of rags to riches that illustrates the importance of strategic data collection and what happens to a team without it. Brigham Frandsen recalls a project that was simultaneously his worst and his best project at McKinsey.

> This particular engagement was almost a textbook example of the pitfalls that result from not consciously following the Rules of Engagement in a study. However, it also demonstrates the rewards that can result from stopping, backing up, and deciding as a team to turn things around. What looked like a disaster of a study turned into one of the highest-impact and most personally rewarding studies during my time at McKinsey.
>
> McKinsey had done a number of highly successful studies with subsidiaries in several countries of a large central European retail-focused bank that resulted in an exponential increase in sales growth. As a result, one affiliate was eager to have us do the same thing for it, and as soon as possible. Thus a team was hurriedly assembled, but it included no engagement manager (there was only a one-year associate who was hoping to make EM), no partner, and nobody who had been involved in the other sales studies. However, eager as we were, the two other associates on the study and I dived in. Going in, we knew little except that we needed to have an implementation plan for

revolutionizing sales and initial impact estimates for a steering committee in two weeks.

We didn't "focus" in terms of data collection—we gathered everything and anything that we could get. As we hadn't framed or organized well, we had no direction for what data to collect. All anyone vaguely knew was that bank affiliates in other countries had had amazing successes in terms of sales increases as a result of these other McKinsey studies, and we wanted to accomplish the same thing. Unfortunately, instead of remedying the problem by leveraging the right expertise, we ran around like headless chickens, interviewing the heck out of the client, asking for its entire data warehouse in Excel format, and putting numbers on charts for the steering committee.

All this came to a head the day before the steering committee meeting, when the absentee partner decided that he wanted to see what he would be helping to present the next day. Not surprisingly, he was not very encouraged by our results thus far. Because of lack of time, he wasn't able to sit down with us to jointly come up with a plan to get the material ready; instead, he got into a yelling match with the aspiring EM, and then gave us associates our orders for the pack, which involved an all-nighter preparing analyses and charts for the next day. That was my worst day and night with McKinsey. The next day, we younger associates were not even invited to the steering committee meeting, which by all accounts didn't go so well anyway—we hadn't gotten any sort of client buy-in ahead of time.

Now, the turnaround. That very afternoon (after the meeting), we sat down as a team (this time with the partner) and slammed the brakes on that runaway train. The very first thing we did was apply the TEAM principles, which we should have done from the beginning. We each took a turn expressing our impressions of what had gone wrong thus far, what our expectations were (as a team and as individuals) for the project, and how to proceed. Among other things, when it was my turn, I said that I absolutely needed to see the end from the beginning (no more blind 10-hour analyses that end up being pointless), and no more all-nighters. I play basketball on Thursdays at 8, and I'm home to put my son to bed at 8:30; if I have to, I'll go back to work when he's asleep.

One result of that team meeting was a feeling on everybody's part that we could make this a rewarding study. More practically, we made a plan to bring in two associate partners who had done similar studies. Within a couple of days, we had a complete framework combining lean banking with sales improvement, and we had the chapters "ghosted" out for the packs for the next two steering committee meetings and the final product, based on that framework. I then took the chapters that I was assigned and literally wrote out all the slides that I would need, complete with titles and ghost charts. In the process of doing this, we were able to clarify the key goals and develop a plan for gathering data, deploying the client team, and getting results. Having this done was extremely empowering for the rest of the study, and we ended up being very successful.

STORY FROM THE FIELD—2

Topic: Working with a large client team helps with data collection as well as buy-in.   Our second story is from an ex-McKinsey consultant who learned about the challenges of working with client team members in data collection and analysis.

For this project team, we had one of the largest groups of client personnel on a project that I ever experienced at McKinsey. The client freed up a significant number of people to work on the project full time, and this large client team ultimately contributed a great deal to the success of the project. Specifically, there were five primary McKinsey people, and each of them led a four- or five-member team of client employees. Because each McKinsey person had to lead a subteam of non-McKinsey people, we all had to do a lot of background work in order to be prepared.

One challenge was that the teams of client employees tended to have low computer, analytical, and data-gathering skills; however, we knew that the only way to succeed was to engage the client, to understand the client, and to build a solution that would work for the client. We were able to accomplish this because there was a great amount of client commitment to achieve those goals.

This commitment and focus on the client team carried over into data collection, deck creation, and project reviews. Normally, in these reviews, the McKinsey team initially maps out the project and gives periodic project updates to senior-level people. This usually takes place in a boardroom, with corporate-level executives and the McKinsey team discussing a slide deck in a vacuum. For this project, though, we decided that it would be necessary to have a more engaging project review. We wanted all the people on the client team to review their findings and to see the progress they were making; it was very helpful for them to see that their senior-level people were responding positively to the work they had done. So, the McKinsey team made a deck, but it also made posters (three or four for each subgroup). The members of the client team then would walk the client leadership through their progress, describe the key findings, and show the data that supported the conclusions.

STORY FROM THE FIELD—BUSINESS SCHOOL EXAMPLE

Topic: Periodically touching base with a partner helps to keep an intern on track with collecting relevant data.   Our business school example comes to us from Ben Kennedy, who interned at a top consulting firm during the summer of his MBA program at the Fuqua School of Business at Duke University. We heard from Ben earlier in Chapter 6, and he dives into the data-collection issues a bit more here.

Our project involved developing a plan for a client that served multiple industries and needed short-term growth. More specifically, our hypothesis was centered on testing a targeted list of industries to determine the highest-priority areas of focus. I was charged with one of three work streams on the project and worked directly with a senior-level partner.

I spent a lot of time gathering and analyzing data. I was able to find many insights in the data on my own, but I really appreciated the discussions with my partner related to the data-collection and analysis process. I would gather and present the data with the partner, and the discussions would help me identify new insights or find holes in my analysis (to be filled by more data). It would obviously have been inefficient to have the partner look at everything I gathered, and identifying what was important was a key part of my job; however, the regular (although brief) update meetings helped keep the research on track.

As another note, during my internship, I also learned how important data are to support a point or, in some cases, refute what you hear in an interview. From time to time, you will get "opinions" during a client interview that ultimately are a bit subjective and not supported by evidence. This may be driven by political issues within the company, and it is important to stay as objective as possible.

CASE STUDY

Tim here. Our case study learned over time that data are the currency of consulting projects.

WHAT WE DID

In our data-collection process, sharing information was invaluable. We introduced a very team-based approach early on in our project with the fact packs we created. We each collected relevant information about our bucket areas in order to help educate the other team members on the basic, important points of each category; that way, everybody had a better understanding of the whole situation. We continued sharing information throughout our project, e-mailing one another relevant articles and other sources that we ran across in our own research. I found that information sharing was even more important in this project than in others I've worked on, because we had, even collectively, virtually no experience with the U.S. city incorporation process. Everything was so new to all of us that it was very important for us to help one another get up to speed.

Another critical component of our information-gathering process was finding a key contact. I managed to find a key contact who had a great depth of experience in precisely the area I was researching (the legal aspects of incorporation and annexation), and I leaned on him heavily for education and references to others with helpful information. He was even able to answer a surprising number of questions for other team members, and his comments helped to keep the entire team moving in the right direction. Sometimes a project requires the collection and synthesis of large amounts of data from diverse sources; other times, a single source serves as the sword that cuts through the Gordian knot. This was an example of the latter.

Alan was also resourceful enough—and lucky enough—to find a great primary resource. He had an experience similar to mine, where his contact either knew the answer to his questions or knew whom to ask. He commented, "We should have gone straight to the source in more situations. One of the biggest takeaways was that we dove into all the FBI and CIA analysis, when we should have called the fire and police chiefs right away and just asked their opinions."

Another helpful practice that we implemented was storing the results of our own research in slide format. As we collected data, we all put it right into slides (instead of Word documents or other formats). This made it very easy for us to share our research and to organize it in such a way that it could be easily found later.

Additionally, we "outsourced" a lot of our research. As I described previously in Chapter 3, we used the Consulting Academy to create subteams that helped us with our research. We all found this to be extremely helpful, but Alan in particular had a very productive week: "Before we went into the academy week, I was spinning my wheels somewhat with all my individual work. Academy week was a great way to get a lot of research done quickly, and we even came out with a lot of slides made."

WHAT I LEARNED

Go to the source! Finding a key contact with deep knowledge about your project's topic is invaluable—especially in a situation like this, where you don't have much prior experience or existing knowledge about your research area. I certainly spent a lot of time becoming familiar with issues and exploring dead ends before I found my key contact. In this project, I realized that people are generally happy to help you, and that it's much easier to find an area expert and ask him or her questions than to try to wade through an abundance of new information yourself.

I will definitely try to be more cognizant of the resources I have at my disposal in the future, and I will push myself to be more creative with them. Using the Consulting Academy students to supplement (and really drive) our research was a huge help, and with our time constraint and the size of our project, it was invaluable.

DELIVERABLES

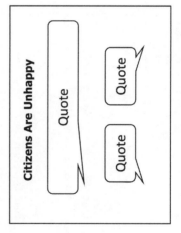

Figure 7-2   Collect: Ghost Charts

143

- Interviewee: Alan Yackey
- Date: January 24, 2007
- Interviewer: Tim
- Topic: Avon example

Background of Interviewee
- Attorney
- Led the incorporation of Avon, Indiana
- Significant experience with annexation in Indiana

Introduction
- Current project overview
- My background
- Purpose and duration of the interview

Key questions to ask
1. How does the annexation process in IN work?
2. Ask about the Avon incorporation example
3. Lessons learned and tips for White River Township

1. **How does the annexation process in IN work?**
   - General overview and history
   - Process steps
   - Legal requirements
2. **The Avon incorporation example**
   - Rationale for incorporation
   - Precise steps and players
   - Documents produced
3. **Lessons learned and tips for White River Township**
   - Discuss hypothesis for Write River Township
   - Seek input as to challenges based on his experiences
   - Jointly develop recommendations for this project

Figure 7-3   Collect: Interview Guide

Key insights:
1. Avon is a relevant example
2. There are several challenges that can be overcome
3. Annexation is a slow and complex process

1. Avon is relevant

- It's recent—1995
- Rationale / motivation for incorporation was better services and more control
  - ➢ Farmers were selling their land to the highest bidder, and the highest bidder was often an irresponsible developer—the development often wasn't what the town had planned or would like to see. If the town had incorporated earlier, it could have prevented much of the bad development with zoning guidelines.
  - ➢ It had crime spilling over from Plainfield.
  - ➢ Wanted to annex 1100 acres in Hendricks County.
- Citizen and government effort led to actual incorporation of a new town
  - ➢ The town didn't annex enough land, though, and it is still dealing with bad development on the outskirts of town. When Avon tries to annex more land, it is annexing poorly developed land, not free land that can be used for business development.

2. There are several challenges that can be overcome

- Lots of analysis necessary
  - ➢ He likened annexation to a business transaction. The problem seems to be that an offer is made, but not accepted by some because it is not explained. The offer needs to be clear, translated into dollars and cents. People respond emotionally to tax issues. Municipalities need to approach them with a benefit-cost analysis.
- Significant communication effort
  - ➢ Those annexations that involved good communication went well, and those that involved poor or nonexistent communication had problems. People should have more power.
  - ➢ Notification and communication with citizens and townships are important.
- Funding for mailings and other process requirements

3. Annexation is a slow and complex process

- It took a long time
  - ➢ The fight lasted more than a year, during which Westfield launched an aggressive campaign to win over landowners.
- Legal requirements
  - ➢ De-annexation is an option if cities fail to provide services within a three-year time frame.
- It would be even longer and more complex for the size of the WRT annexation
  - ➢ Approximately 10–30 times as large

Figure 7-4 Collect: Interview Summary

145

Competitor Data

- **Factiva**
  - ➤ General news
  - ➤ Detailed company reports
  - ➤ Daily newspapers

- **Mergent Online**
  - ➤ Deep data on firms
  - ➤ Downlowdable financials

- **Hoovers Online**
  - ➤ Company profiles
  - ➤ Comprehensive reports

Industry Data

- **Datamonitor**
  - ➤ Consumer market reports
  - ➤ Quick hits on key trends within the industries

- **S&P NetAdvantage**
  - ➤ Outstanding industry data
  - ➤ Company comparisons and industry outlooks

- **Frost & Sullivan**
  - ➤ Full industry reports
  - ➤ International coverage

Market Trends

- **Reuters Business Insight**
  - ➤ Global market reports
  - ➤ Includes health care, IT, transportation, etc.

- **Investext Plus**
  - ➤ Full–text research reports
  - ➤ Prepared by industry research specialists

- **Government Data**
  - ➤ Census.gov
  - ➤ Fedstats.gov
  - ➤ BLS.gov

Figure 7-5   Collect: Key Secondary Sources

8

UNDERSTAND

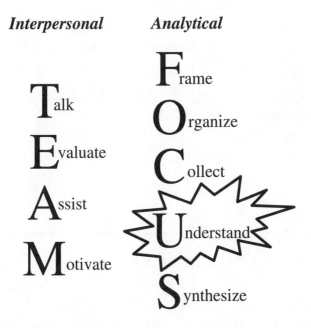

Figure 8-1   TEAM FOCUS Model—Understand

CONCEPT

This chapter addresses the real value that a consultant adds to a project—identifying the takeaways from data collection. The magic is then converting them into meaningful insights that form the essence of the answer to the key question. If the team has been following the scientific method as described in previous chapters, this is the stage where the original hypotheses are either supported or refuted. In most cases, the hypotheses are modified as the insights flow in, and these refined hypotheses become the ultimate recommendations that are presented to the client, which are discussed in detail in the next chapter.

The biggest challenge that teams face in the Understanding phase is developing the highest-quality insights. Teams describe this part as "hurting a little" from a mental perspective, as it requires additional processing power. The Rules of Engagement and Operating Tactics described in this chapter all provide guidance that is designed to make the Understand element as effective as possible. It is critical to build the right answer for the client based upon the supporting data and intuitive observations.

RULES OF ENGAGEMENT

You have gathered a lot of data and information, and much of it appears to have relevance to the key question. Now, the team must digest the data and articulate the insights that will eventually become the basis for the final recommendations. The Rules of Engagement for doing this as efficiently as possible are given here.

RULE 1: IDENTIFY THE "SO WHAT(S)"

Two of the most important words within McKinsey are "so what?" This term has immediate connotations of testing the relevance of the data that have been gathered for a particular study. To operationalize this concept, it may be helpful to ask and answer one of three questions: "What is the impact of this insight on the project team's tentative answer?" "Will this insight change the direction of our analysis?" and/or "Will implementation of this insight ultimately have a material impact on the client's operations?" The answer to the questions will ultimately be the answer—or the "so what."

At McKinsey, team members would typically ask each other "so what?" many times every day as they sorted through the myriad of data available for analysis. When the team is struggling to find an answer, it is quite likely that the data and the insights currently associated with them may not be very important, and that they could be a candidate for the appendix or the pile of interesting but irrelevant data and insights.

RULE 2: THINK THROUGH THE IMPLICATIONS FOR ALL CONSTITUENTS

This Rule of Engagement is closely related to the first rule, but it goes even further in specificity. The questions in the first rule have a yes/no answer regarding the relevance of the insight for the project—especially in terms of the client. The implications analysis in this rule goes deeper into the potential impact and broadens the scope of the investigation beyond just the immediate client.

So who are the different constituents who should be considered in a consulting project? Essentially, there are three groups:

- *The consulting team.* As you sort through your data to understand each "so what," the first constituent group to consider is your fellow consultants. In addition to helping to check the validity and thoroughness of your tentative understandings, your coworkers may be affected by the implications of these understandings for their particular areas of analysis. No matter how hard the team strives to maintain independent and MECE streams of analysis, there will undoubtedly be overlaps. So, the team members continually check in with one another to share implications.

- *The client project team.* The most obvious implications for the client project team (which includes the high-level sponsor, the key point of contact, and anyone assigned to work on the project with the consulting team) are the answers to the key question. Less obvious implications for consideration include political issues (promotion plans, informal rules of communication, and unspoken influence tactics), answers to different but related questions (possible future consulting projects), and private agendas (remember, the people you are working with have been attempting change efforts well before you arrived).

- *The client implementation team:* One of the biggest criticisms of consulting firms (especially McKinsey at one time) is their inability or unwillingness to consider implementation in their recommendations. The truth of the matter is that providing great ideas that cannot realistically be implemented is as ineffective as not even doing the work (and more costly!). During a project, it is important to think through how the recommendations will be carried out, who will be doing the implementation, and what needs to be addressed to ensure that the implementation will actually happen.

RULE 3: DOCUMENT THE KEY INSIGHT ON ALL CHARTS

The final Rule of Engagement involves the explicit documentation of the insight on each and every slide. I would like to first discuss the reasons why this is so important and then cover some tips for doing it well.

The Collecting and Understanding processes are designed to work hand in hand during the team's problem-solving journey. The team sketches out the story line, drafts ghost slides, gathers the data to fill in the charts, and then finalizes the insight statement on each chart. This is the most important part of the process. McKinsey typically inserts the insight at the top of each slide in the form of a sentence. Other firms place the key insight somewhere else on the page and use the top of the slide as the tracker or section divider (our approach will be covered more thoroughly in the next chapter). This statement is extremely important to the process, as it makes explicit the reason why the chart exists and shares that reason with the rest of the team, and eventually with the client.

A few tips for identifying and documenting the insight on each slide are (1) start early, (2) seek input, and (3) think in terms of impact for the client. In terms of timing, the first draft of the insight statement is actually prepared before any data are gathered. As described in the previous chapter, the ghost slide has a tentative insight into what the data may ultimately support (kind of a mini-hypothesis). The insight statement may evolve a bit as the data are collected—it is always important to ensure that the statement is supported by the data and does not make claims beyond what the data support. The insight-generation process is so important that it should not be left to one person. Research shows that diversity of opinion leads to better answers, so you should seek input from other team members as you develop your insights and test them with supporting data. The processes of seeking others' input and describing your assumptions lead to better charts and insights.

Finally, all insights should eventually be tied to some impact for the client. Remember, that is why we are here! One way to do this is to identify the specific impact that the insight has on the eventual recommendation, and how that recommendation, in turn, affects the client's operations. Every McKinsey engagement includes quantification of the potential impact for the client (especially because this is part of the firm's core mission statement). Typically, this will be in the form of additional revenue or decreased costs and will include an explicit statement of assumptions as well as a range estimate for the quantified impact.

OPERATING TACTICS

The Operating Tactics for the Understand element of the TEAM FOCUS model are:

- *Tactic 35:* Ask "so what?" to sort through the analysis to find out what is ultimately important.
- *Tactic 36:* Estimate the impact of the recommendations on the client's operations.

STORIES FROM THE FIELD

STORY FROM THE FIELD—1

Topic: A client's failure to communicate changes in expectations effectively leads to an abrupt change of direction for the consultant team. D. A. Gros saw many successful projects during his tenure at McKinsey and recalls how important understanding and adapting to the client perspective was during one project that he supervised.

On a pharmaceutical project, as a senior engagement manager, I was in charge of a team that was to help the company develop a pure growth strategy for its Asia-Pacific market. This included brainstorming on strategy for 10 different countries and checking in with the head of the Asia-Pacific region, who was based in the United States.

On a Friday two weeks into the project, when we were delivering the draft book for review, the senior client executive flipped through the book and suddenly threw it back across the table at me, stating that it was all wrong. Four weeks before the start of the project, I had discussed the project's direction with both the McKinsey partners and the client—it was to be a pure growth-strategy engagement. However, in the six weeks that had passed since that meeting, developments in the market and within the company had created significant financial pressures that required a cost-reduction strategy rather than a growth strategy.

Because of this new direction, we had to reevaluate the company's position, go back to the drawing board, and start over with the Frame process. One of the first things I did was to reach out to the partner on the project and discuss this change in direction. By the day after the disastrous meeting, I had spoken with several McKinsey experts on cost reduction and read relevant white papers—by leveraging the subject-matter experts, I became very proficient in the cost-reduction matters we would be addressing. By Saturday evening, my team was plowing through this problem from the new angle.

After burning the midnight oil for several days, we had a new deck prepared for a Tuesday meeting. This time, the senior executive was very satisfied with the result, and the project was extended for Asia and eventually led to further work in Latin America.

STORY FROM THE FIELD—2

Topic: Understanding the "so whats" is at the heart of a consul-tant's advice for project success.   Mike Yang offers the following bits of advice from his McKinsey days:

- *"So what."* A story is not a story without the "so what"; it proves the importance of the insight and translates it into impact for clients.
- *Implications for constituents.* In addition to considering the constituents, you need to make sure that you validate the insights through private syndication. If you have a gut feeling that someone will not like the result, that person probably won't. It's better to prepare the various constituents for discussions and ask them for input ahead of time than to have unpleasant surprises in subsequent meetings.
- *Document the key insight.* Each chart should have a clear and meaningful point. If you can't find that point, then this probably is not a good chart—remove it from the deck.

STORY FROM THE FIELD—BUSINESS SCHOOL EXAMPLE:

Topic: Understanding other team members' roles and assignments helps a team to conduct a successful engagement efficiently.   While working as an associate at McKinsey, one MBA interviewee experienced the worst-to-best team project in which he has ever participated.

My project started out terribly wrong. The engagement manager was not able to meet until two weeks into the study. As a result, I was the lone wolf. Accordingly,

I gathered as much data as I could find from past McKinsey studies, industry reports, and recent articles.

My pride in the 200-page slide deck was destroyed at my first progress meeting with the engagement manager. She must have said "so what" 180 times as she literally tore each irrelevant slide out of the deck and threw it to the floor. It was a long and painful meeting.

The study took a positive turn when the partner met with us the next day and together we clarified the story line and role each of us would play, and expanded our team size. With increased focus on the right issues and better-directed resources, the project got completely turned around.

CASE STUDY

I will never forget the importance of "so whats" in team problem solving.

WHAT WE DID

One of our most important guiding principles was to focus on the "so whats" of our analysis. Dr. Friga had drilled so-what thinking into our heads before the project ever started, so we didn't have much trouble remembering to focus on the relevance of the information we had gathered. The tricky part of this project lay in determining the effects of the conclusions each member reached on other members' project elements. For instance, there was a tension between the "finances" and "autonomy" buckets: by incorporating as a stand-alone community, Center Grove would have a great deal of autonomy, but it would be strapped financially for at least two years. On the other hand, incorporation into another community by way of annexation would solve a lot of the financial and logistical problems, but it would sacrifice much of the community's freedom to pursue its own objectives in taxing and spending.

Another of our success factors was applying this so-what thinking on a broader level. We didn't just think about how the data were relevant to us or to our project; we also considered the implications of our findings for the constituents—we basically tried to put ourselves in their shoes, and then ask, "So what?" While we understood (more or less) where the constituents were coming from, it was still difficult for us to construct our presentation, since we knew that the audience probably wouldn't be overly receptive to any type of change. Because the constituents were all so personally invested in the decision regarding incorporation, annexation, or doing nothing, certain members of the audience proved to be very hostile. For example, even though we anticipated that people would not be excited about a tax increase and we tried to mitigate its negative connotations by emphasizing other positive effects, most people were still adamantly opposed to any sort of tax increase. Several in attendance were ultimately convinced of a new perspective by our presentation; especially poignant was the example of an older woman who mentioned that she had a change of heart after seeing our data and considering the impact on her grandchildren and great-grandchildren.

WHAT I LEARNED

Data are necessary to form conclusions, and it is certainly necessary to back them up; however, just presenting a lot of information is useless. Furthermore, it's generally not a good idea to just present a lot of information and let the audience draw its own conclusions. This project really enforced how important it is to come up with a single viable solution and present a clear point of view, so that the audience isn't left confused. This is something that I think applies to any project, as you will always want to make sure that your audience gets the most it can out of your presentation. The best way to ensure that you don't leave your audience members hanging short of a solid conclusion and asking itself, "So what?" is to present clear solutions and relevant so-whats to them.

DELIVERABLES

Constituent	Implications / Concerns
WRT Citizens	■ New insights based on analysis ■ Long-term considerations for their future concerns over tax increases
Johnson County Leaders	■ Document for use in strategic discussions ■ Clarity over potential role in the process
Kelley School of Business	Students: ■ Application of business school tools ■ Development of presentation skills ■ Impact on the community Kelley: ■ Alignment with the university mission of outreach and impact on Indiana communities ■ Potential differentiation as a contributing business school

Figure 8-2 Understand: Implications Summary

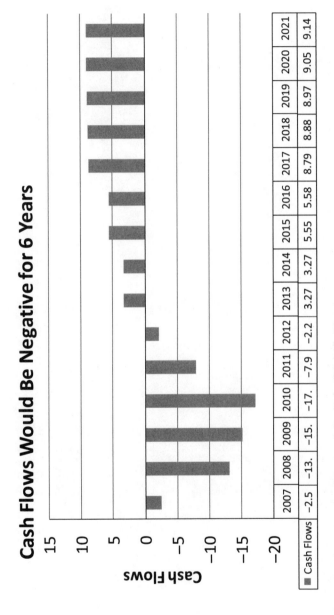

Cash Flows Would Be Negative for 6 Years

	2007	2008	2009	2010	2011	2012	2013	2014	2015	2016	2017	2018	2019	2020	2021
Cash Flows	-2.5	-13.	-15.	-17.	-7.9	-2.2	3.27	3.27	5.55	5.58	8.79	8.88	8.97	9.05	9.14

Figure 8-3   Understand: Insight-Titled Chart

9

SYNTHESIZE

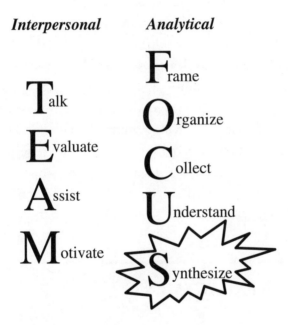

Figure 9-1 TEAM FOCUS Model—Synthesize

CONCEPT

This final chapter is dedicated to the three people within McKinsey who influenced me the most in terms of developing the material for this book: Harry Langstaff, Gene Zelazny, and Barbara Minto.

Harry was the heart and soul of the introductory training program at McKinsey, during which all new associates would travel to rural England to learn and practice many of the McKinsey principles of teamwork and analysis. He passed away in 2006, but I will never forget his command of core McKinsey ideas, his uncanny knowledge of methodologies, and his personal touch. Gene Zelazny is the mastermind behind McKinsey's ability to transfer outstanding ideas into compelling charts and graphics.

Last but certainly not least is Barbara Minto, who completely changed the way thousands of consultants and executives (at McKinsey and elsewhere) do analysis and deliver recommendations. Her work within McKinsey, and now with her own consulting firm, is world renowned, and her books are required reading for every student I teach. Her ideas are the backbone of efficient and effective team problem solving, and they are described in more detail within this chapter.

RULES OF ENGAGEMENT

The Rules of Engagement for this chapter all relate to developing and delivering a good argument—well structured and well delivered. It is important to remember that the best way to accomplish this feat is through team coordination, which always trumps individual efforts (and comes with its own set of challenges, of course).

RULE 1: OBTAIN INPUT AND ENSURE "BUY-IN" FROM THE CLIENT

One of the most important operating assumptions for successful consulting engagements is to engage the client actively. Popular press stories of McKinsey being a firm that comes in with a fantastic strategy slide deck that cannot be implemented are unfounded. In fact, in every project at McKinsey, the team is charged with actively involving the client throughout the entire process and never completing a project without a detailed implementation plan and a specific understanding of the impact that the changes will have on the organization.

The motivation for client involvement is quite clear and is related to the twofold mission statement that is documented in every one of McKinsey's 90+ offices around the world: (1) help leaders make distinctive, lasting, and substantial improvements to the performance of their organizations and (2) provide our people with an outstanding place to work, with opportunities for growth that they can find nowhere else. The leaders of McKinsey's client companies must take an active role during any McKinsey study. They provide perspectives and knowledge that are available nowhere else, they know the culture of the company, and they will ultimately be in charge of implementing the ideas and making positive changes in their respective organizations.

There are several opportunities for client engagement that need to be strategically managed to ensure that effective problem solving takes place. In addition to the eventual impact the recommendations may have in terms of organizational performance, the short-term performance indicator is whether or not there is client "buy-in" to the recommendations. Without such acceptance, there is no chance of successful implementation.

- *Before the engagement.* McKinsey does not undertake an engagement without substantial discussions with the client sponsor to ensure that the business problem is well defined, that there is a chance for substantial performance improvement, and that the client will be adequately

involved during the project. This understanding is also
documented in the letter of agreement (see Chapter 5).

- *During the engagement.* Interviews are a significant
  opportunity for client involvement and buy-in. The interview list is critical; the team must make sure that the key
  knowledge holders, political constituents, and ultimate
  implementers are included. Note that the interviews are not
  just about gathering data, but also about testing hypotheses
  and building relationships. Progress meetings are also held,
  where draft recommendations, findings, and data are shared
  to ensure that the project is headed in the right direction in
  an efficient manner. There should be no surprises in the final
  meeting with the client—just positive energy and discussions
  of implementation plans and their impact.

- *After the engagement.* The best consulting firms all realize
  that consulting projects are more often sold on a relationship basis than as one-off RFPs (requests for proposal).
  The key is maintaining a long-term relationship. At
  McKinsey, this is a high priority, and every client has a
  relationship partner who gets to know the top management team and follows up after projects to ensure that the
  projects had impact and to discuss other ways to continue
  to help the clients achieve their business objectives.

RULE 2: OFFER SPECIFIC RECOMMENDATIONS FOR IMPROVEMENT

This Rule of Engagement is a reminder to keep in mind why
consultants are here in the first place: to help clients. While it may
be obvious that the hypotheses that drive our analysis become
recommendations after they are proven, the high level of specificity
required is not obvious. This is an area in which junior consultants

often struggle as they craft recommendations for the final slide deck.

As will be described later in this chapter, every final set of recommendations should have a governing point. This could be anchored in the general kind of change that the organization is pursuing (a change in strategic positioning, operational improvements, increased knowledge sharing, cost reductions, or some other area), the financial impact of the changes suggested, or some other organizing construct.

The next level down should capture a more specific set of recommendations (generally no more than three). The engagement's findings will provide the rationale for these recommendations, and the proposed tactics will supply an execution plan. Each project may have its own particular set of recommendations, but the action steps will generally be supported by information about why and how. We will cover the topic of how to craft and deliver the story in the next section.

RULE 3: TELL A GOOD STORY

Now, at the end of the project, it's time to craft the final argument, right? Wrong! As we have discussed, you and your team should have been working on the overall argument and support since the beginning of the process (as described in Chapter 5). The story is iterative, and by the end of the project, it will have developed and morphed into findings, conclusions, and ultimately recommendations based upon the testing described in Chapters 6 through 8.

The "story" concept is common nomenclature within McKinsey—every project has a story (or overall "argument"), and it starts with the basic components that all stories share: situation, complication, and resolution. The team has to figure out the situation and complication (suggested in part by the engagement letter), then develop and test hypotheses to determine the resolution. More thinking up front in terms of strategic framing and organizing leads to more efficient data collection (as you are more focused and gather less irrelevant data). The original intention of the story (and the manner in which Barbara Minto teaches the concept) refers only to the introduction. The reader is likely to know the situation and complication in advance, and the resolution is the answer to the key question.

Barbara Minto's teaching within McKinsey has created a strong culture of professionals who are extremely adept at doing efficient analysis by constantly thinking in a pyramid manner. She also emphasizes how important it is to communicate carefully with the client. One of the key tenets of her philosophy (and McKinsey's) is to begin with the recommendations (there are times when buildup is necessary because of the sensitivity of the conclusions, but those are rare), followed by supporting findings, data, and tactics. This contrasts with the way in which many consultants, executives, and students traditionally present, which is more along the lines of situation, analysis, findings, and recommendations. If you keep your audience in mind, McKinsey's approach makes sense; as an audience member, you would appreciate the reverse order, which gets right to the main point, supported by conclusions and facts. This presentation format is easier to digest and thus creates a better product.

One of my favorite (and very simple) examples that makes this point is taken from Barbara Minto's bestselling book, *The Minto Pyramid Principle: Logic in Writing, Thinking and Problem Solving*, which she has graciously agreed to allow me to reproduce here:

Have you ever received or even written a message like this?

> *"John Collins telephoned to say that he can't make the meeting at 3:00. Hal Johnson says he doesn't mind making it*

later, or even tomorrow, but not before 10:30, and Don Clifford's secretary says that Clifford won't return from Frankfurt until tomorrow, late. The Conference Room is booked tomorrow, but free Thursday. Thursday at 11:00 looks to be a good time. Is that OK for you?"

If you present the main point first followed by support-ing data, it would look like the message shown below.

"Could we reschedule today's meeting to Thursday at 11:00? This would be more convenient for Collins and Johnson, and would also permit Clifford to be present."

Can you see (and appreciate) the difference? You can imagine how significant it becomes with a 50-page slide deck that follows a three-month, $3 million project.

The magic of organizing the ideas in the pyramid properly takes work and is iterative. There are three rules to keep in mind as you work out the structure of your ideas (also reprinted with the permission of Barbara Minto):

1. Ideas at any level must be summaries of the ideas grouped below them
2. Ideas in each grouping must be logically the same
3. Ideas in each grouping must be in logical order

I have also found a few additional pieces of advice helpful for students and consultants who are learning to employ this approach:

- *Always focus on your audience.* Learn as much as you can about your client, including but not limited to his or her education, tenure in the organization, title, preferences, and possible reactions to the recommendations (negative, neutral, or positive). Adjust accordingly!

- *Speak the language of the client.* Many clients actually have a disdain for "consulting speak" and prefer outsiders who learn to speak the language of the host company. This includes very careful control over early drafts of the story and recommendations, and perhaps not using the term *hypothesis* too much. (I have seen clients react negatively to this term, as they sometimes think you are forcing an early answer to their problem without adequate analysis.)
- *Utilize a flexible presentation approach.* Presentations and meetings have heterogeneous audiences with different backgrounds and preferences. It is important to balance slide decks and presentations to offer something for everyone. The beauty of the pyramid principle is that it allows you to do just that by providing a high-level message and loads of detail at different levels as well.

OPERATING TACTICS

The Operating Tactics for the Synthesize element of the TEAM FOCUS model are:

- *Tactic 37:* Tell a story—use a very brief situation and complication followed by the resolution, which is the most important aspect of the project.
- *Tactic 38:* Share the story with the client and the team ahead of time to obtain input and ensure buy-in.
- *Tactic 39:* Keep the story simple, and focus on the original problem and specific recommendations for improvement; include the estimated impact on the organization.
- *Tactic 40:* Have fun!

STORIES FROM THE FIELD

STORY FROM THE FIELD—1

Topic: Thinking through the end presentation leads to more efficient problem solving.   Our first story comes from a friend of mine who was a partner at Deloitte and later at Infosys Consulting, where he encountered an engagement that was spiraling out of control until the pyramid principle saved the day.

> I was the partner for an IT cost-effectiveness engagement for a large, global auto supplier based in Europe. Our objective was to assess the client's information technology costs and to recommend changes. As you can imagine, this was a very sensitive assignment in a company with a decentralized management organization. The consulting team quickly got into the weeds by reviewing a ton of cost information in multiple spreadsheets, reports, and online databases before we had really organized our thinking. We needed to step back and get focused!
>
> We began to organize our thinking along the lines of what we would ultimately present to the client. We employed the situation-complication-resolution approach. The situation was a client with a strong business model. With a little industry research, we found that the complication was that the client spent significantly more than its competitors on information technology as a percentage of revenue. The key question was how better to align its spending with competitors', and our recommendation was that the client reduce IT spending by 30 percent while maintaining or improving service levels to the organization.

Expanding this structure led to defining multiple subquestions, each of which had multiple hypotheses regarding recommendations to accomplish the goal. Our data collection either proved or disproved these hypotheses, and the proven ones became recommendations for action. The benefit of using this logical breakdown was twofold. First, it organized our thinking, focused our data collection on testing the hypotheses, and ensured that we covered the issues in a mutually exclusive, collectively exhaustive manner. Second, in presenting the results to the client's management team, the logic of our approach clearly explained our conclusions in a way that was more acceptable given the controversial nature of some of our recommendations.

STORY FROM THE FIELD—2

Topic: Identifying and involving the right client constituents during the engagement process helps an engagement run smoothly.   Arnaud Beernaert recalls how important buy-in is from an early study during his days at McKinsey.

As you're working toward an extremely tight deadline and refining your analysis or adding a few more exhibits to back up your thesis, you run the risk of forgetting that this next progress review, for which you are putting together an impressive deck, can end up being a complete failure if you haven't taken the time to achieve some prior buy-in. It's a bit like imagining that you could make your way through a minefield without a map. This is the type of material step that is easily overlooked by a junior consultant. It becomes more and more critical the larger the number of people attending and the larger the number of hidden agendas.

I remember one of my first engagements as a manager, where we had been mandated to reassess the product mix and go-to-market approach for a corporate banking division of a major European financial player. Not only was that project particularly difficult to structure, as it covered many different issues, but it was also a real challenge to manage, as there were so many constituents. It wasn't too difficult to convince the division head, who had asked us to come in the first place, but there were many key employees under him who proved much more difficult to win over and who could have completely derailed the process if they had wanted to do so.

The up-front identification of these employees was not obvious, as they included not only the key people in the hierarchy, but also some regular salespeople who were extremely influential (something that we were not aware of initially). I ended up putting an incredible amount of my time into talking to some of these guys, making sure that I understood exactly where they came from, what their vision was, and on what basis it had been formed. The associate partner and I had to keep them in the loop constantly in order to make sure that they were aligned with our thinking, and we frequently sat down with them in one-on-one meetings between progress reviews to make sure that we had ironed everything out beforehand. As time-intensive as this was, it was the only way to achieve buy-in and to avoid explosions and uncontrolled debate during the reviews.

STORY FROM THE FIELD—3
Topic: Application of the pyramid structure is a key takeaway from one consultant's career at McKinsey.   Ken Shachmut, who is

now implementing many lessons from McKinsey as the senior vice president in charge of strategic initiatives at Safeway, shows just how much impact Barbara Minto's theories had on him.

> I recall three very important lessons that the firm taught and reinforced: (1) analytical rigor, (2) intense focus on what is important to the business and the CEO, and (3) intellectual honesty. In addition, I have to say that perhaps the most significant takeaway for me was a result of the value the firm places on high-quality written and oral communications. The pyramid structure, as taught in the gospel according to Barbara Minto, is the backbone of good analysis and presentations at McKinsey. I use pyramid structure routinely today and expect it from my staff.

STORY FROM THE FIELD—BUSINESS SCHOOL EXAMPLE

Topic: Buy-in from a key member of the client team drives efficient engagement work and ensures positive client reception of the recommendation.   Our last story from the field comes from a very special student with whom I worked at the Kelley School of Business at Indiana University. Peter Kuo was my research assistant and an amazing leader during his MBA program. He was a star in the program (especially on case competitions and field studies), and he is headed for great things with McKinsey in Atlanta after graduation.

> At the start of my second year in the MBA program at the Kelley School of Business, Dr. Friga selected me to work with a student team for a weeklong pro bono project with McKinsey & Company and the Metro Atlanta YMCA. The YMCA gave us the task of developing a membership growth strategy that would capitalize on the cross-channel

conversion of temporary program members to stable facility members. We wanted to make a difference for the YMCA, so we focused on delivering a solution that it could implement given its resources and constraints. Throughout the course of the week, we looked to several resources for direction.

While primary research and data analysis were both important, perhaps the most valuable resource was the client—Betsy, the marketing director for the YMCA. Betsy knew the situation better than we did: who the key decision makers were, and what barriers we would face with any given recommendation. We worked with Betsy every step of the way, and she helped us access people and data, identify workable solutions, and devise the optimal package of solutions for the YMCA. In short, synthesis would not have been possible without obtaining the participation and buy-in of the client.

As we prepared for the final presentation, we tailored our story to the expected audience. Betsy and our supervising manager at McKinsey both informed us that the audience would consist of various members at different levels of the YMCA organization (from facility management to the CEO) and of McKinsey (an engagement manager, an associate partner, and a director). Not having prior buy-in from many in the audience, we decided to build up to our recommendation by first providing the background information and context to get the audience up to speed.

Our presentation was a success. The most compelling part of our story was Betsy and her incredible enthusiasm for our plan. By working with us closely throughout the process, she became a champion for our recommendations, giving our presentation greater credibility. What we learned was simple: buy-in is important. Ultimately, the YMCA took one of our recommendations and ran with it, and McKinsey started another pro bono study to follow up on that recommendation.

Our last report out on the case study reveals several important lessons learned the "hard" way: (1) work on the overall argument earlier in the process; (2) document and share your slides on a regular basis; and (3) don't wait until the last minute to finalize your slide deck!

CASE STUDY

WHAT WE DID

Even though we had been very organized throughout our research process, we still had to struggle to get everyone's relevant information into slide format, and then to get all those slides together in a timely fashion. Shalini and Rachita volunteered to put together a slide deck, gathering everybody's individual slides and compiling them into a logical, coherent, cohesive presentation. However, we were all somewhat reluctant to relinquish control and wanted to finalize our own slides—I remember Rachita saying it was "like pulling teeth" to get us to actually send her our slides. They eventually had to call us and tell us to just send them our slides, whether they were completely finished or not.

Once we had finally sent our slides to Rachita and Shalini, they spent a lot of time wrestling with the flow of the story. Even though we had all been collectively refining our story throughout the research process, it still wasn't clear how to present the story so that it would flow best. One issue we had to consider was the receptiveness of the audience; as we thought the audience might be hostile, we wanted to build to our point, rather than attack people with it right off the bat. Dr. Friga expressed reservations about ending with bad news (higher taxes), but ultimately we decided to build to our recommendation and to its implications. Another decision we made was to present each of our bucket issues separately (rather than telling a more streamlined story that incorporated components of each bucket throughout). By presenting separate issues independently, the audience could more easily think about how incorporation or annexation would affect each category.

Looking back at our Synthesize phase, I am immediately reminded of our hectic last-minute preparation. We were working right up to our deadline, not in the sense that our data were coming in late, but in the sense that we were putting the physical deliverables together right up until the very end. Dr. Friga wanted to review the slide deck we came up with, and he ended up changing a lot of the slides (both their content and their order). Since he received the final slide deck so late, he sent out the revised slides about an hour before the presentation, and so there was no time to practice at all. It seems funny now, but when we were driving to the presentation with Bhavin reading the slides to the driver while the other team members were compiling and organizing papers in the back, we were very stressed and less than amused. I guess this is one of the experiences Dr. Friga was referring to when he said that this would be "real life."

Despite our last-minute preparation and our inability to even run through our final slides together, our presentation went remarkably well. However, we were absolutely bombarded with questions from the audience. It was very hard for many members of the audience to separate their emotions from the facts—it was even more of a personal, emotionally charged issue than we had realized. One of my greatest learning experiences during the project came from watching how Dr. Friga defended our presentation while the audience was growing more and more emotional—he made his points, but he didn't argue, and he knew when to let go and move on. The ideas were supported by facts, and the clarity of the argument won many people over that day.

WHAT I LEARNED

During this project, I realized that even when you think you know the story you're going to tell, actually putting the slides in order and making them flow well can be a challenge. Conveying your story well in a slide deck really is an art, and it is an art that takes more time than you think. In the future, I'll definitely budget more time for the preparation of the final slide deck.

I also learned (out of necessity, really) that it is possible to present well without practice and under stressful circumstances, but it is certainly not preferable! It can be exciting to work under a time crunch, and stress can be a great motivator, but in the future I will plan to be scrambling less at the end of a project.

CG2020

A Study on the Incorporation of Center Grove

Dr. Paul N. Friga
Alan Burleson
Chris Cannon
Tim Krzywicki
Shalini Makkar
Bhavin Shah
Rachita Sundar

April 24, 2007

This study is a pro bono effort and was created for academic purposes. The report is part of a much larger discussion; assumptions have been made and data gathered for analysis where available. Please do not cite or use without permission of Dr. Paul N. Friga.

Figure 9-2 Synthesize: Final Report

The story at a glance

- **Introduction**
  - ➤ A team of Kelley faculty and students investigated incorporation options for Center Grove
  - ➤ The pro bono study spanned one year and included primary and secondary research
  - ➤ Center Grove is an upscale community with many strengths, but it faces several challenges due to dramatic growth——it should consider annexation or incorporation

- **Conclusion**
  - ➤ Incorporation could improve the safety and condition of roads
  - ➤ Incorporation could provide upgrades to important services such as police, waste, and water
  - ➤ Incorporation could allow more local control over zoning and lead to more green space and economic development

- **Implementation**
  - ➤ An incorporation would take several years but would have positive long-term impact
  - ➤ Incorporation could be financially feasible with funding through loans and bonds; it would require an increase in certain taxes
  - ➤ There are risks and challenges to completing the incorporation

Figure 9-2   Synthesize: Final Report (*continued*)

The story at a glance

■ **Introduction**

 ➤ A team of Kelley faculty and students investigated incorporation options for Center Grove
 ➤ The pro bono study spanned one year and included primary and secondary research
 ➤ Center Grove is an upscale community with many strengths, but it faces several challenges due to dramatic growth—it should consider annexation or incorporation

■ **Conclusion**

 ➤ Incorporation could improve the safety and condition of roads
 ➤ Incorporation could provide upgrades to important services such as police, waste, and water
 ➤ Incorporation could allow more local control over zoning and lead to more green space and economic development

■ **Implementation**

 ➤ An incorporation would take several years but would have positive long-term impact
 ➤ Incorporation could be financially feasible with funding through loans and bonds; it would require an increase in certain taxes
 ➤ There are risks and challenges to completing the incorporation

Figure 9-2   Synthesize: Final Report (*continued*)

179

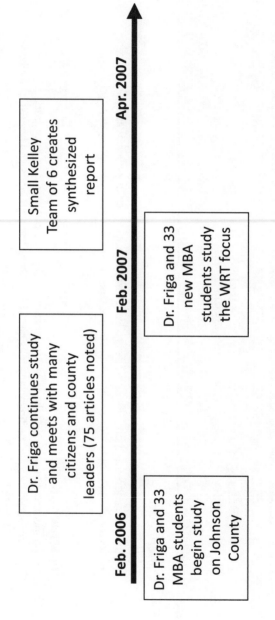

Figure 9-2 Synthesize: Final Report (*continued*)

WRT is known for higher income and property values

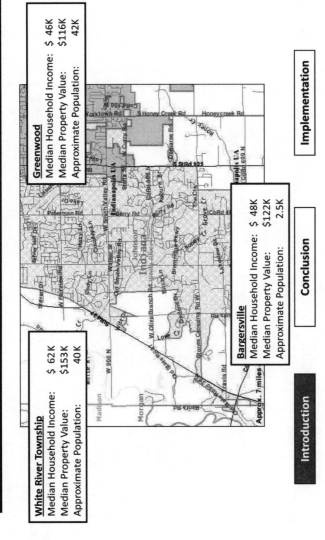

White River Township
Median Household Income: $ 62K
Median Property Value: $153K
Approximate Population: 40 K

Greenwood
Median Household Income: $ 46K
Median Property Value: $116K
Approximate Population: 42K

Bargersville
Median Household Income: $ 48K
Median Property Value: $122K
Approximate Population: 2.5K

Introduction   Conclusion   Implementation

Source: U.S. Census and City Web sites.

Figure 9-2 Synthesize: Final Report (*continued*)

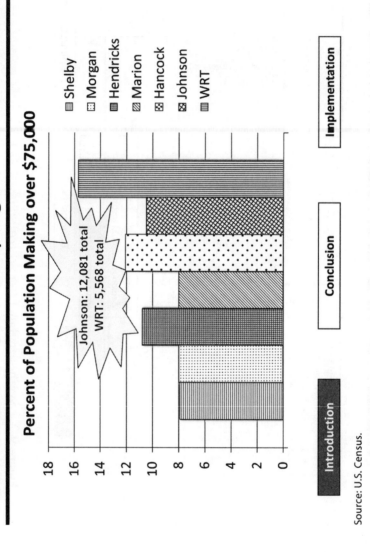

Source: U.S. Census.

Figure 9-2 Synthesize: Final Report (*continued*)

The Center Grove area boasts attractive demographics

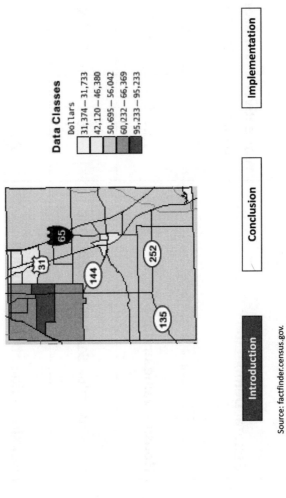

Source: factfinder.census.gov.

Figure 9-2 Synthesize: Final Report (*continued*)

WRT homes are a cut above

General Demographic Characteristic	White River Township	Johnson County	State of Indiana
Housing value under $100,000	12.7%	31.5%	55.3%
Housing value $100,000—$200,000	61.6%	54.7%	36.4%
Housing value above $200,000	25.6%	13.8%	8.3%

Introduction   Conclusion   Implementation

Source: www.centergrove.k12.in.us.

Figure 9-2 Synthesize: Final Report (*continued*)

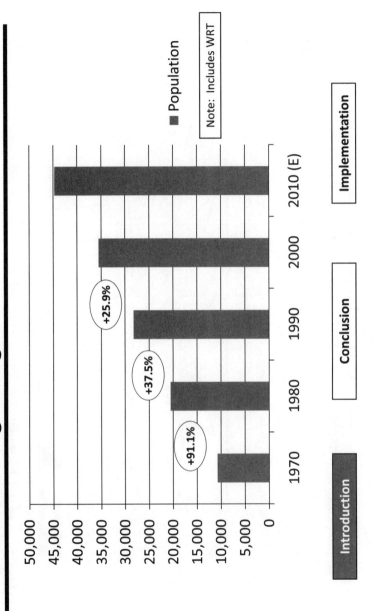

Figure 9-2 Synthesize: Final Report (*continued*)

185

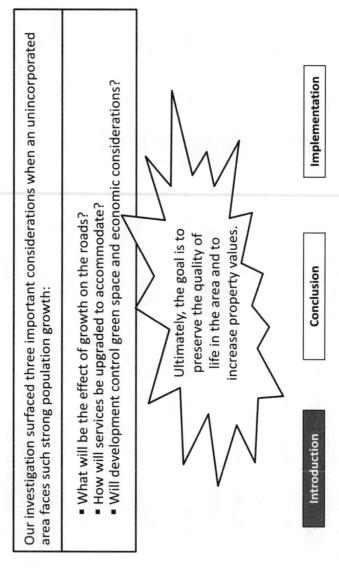

We targeted three primary issues for investigation

Our investigation surfaced three important considerations when an unincorporated area faces such strong population growth:

- What will be the effect of growth on the roads?
- How will services be upgraded to accommodate?
- Will development control green space and economic considerations?

Ultimately, the goal is to preserve the quality of life in the area and to increase property values.

Introduction   Conclusion   Implementation

Figure 9-2 Synthesize: Final Report (*continued*)

We considered several incorporation options

Option	Pro	Con	Comment
Status quo—remain unincorporated	No time, energy, or additional resources needed	Significant concerns over handling growth and preserving property values	Investigate further through this study and consider Carmel and Avon examples
Annex with Greenwood	Less administrative infrastructure needed	Greenwood would grow to double its current size and has not expressed interest in such a move	Has promise but would require a significant shift in strategy from Greenwood and may lead to CG resistance
Annex with Bargersville	Could build off of existing police, waste, and water services	Would require a dramatic change in government structure—20X growth would be tough (and largest annexation in IN history)	Bargersville may be interested, but it would take a long time and may be met with CG resistance
Incorporate as new city	Fresh start allows for strategic control over destiny	Would require visionary leadership and significant investment as well as creation of a new tax structure	Concern that citizens will be resistant to change and miss the opportunity for long-term improvements

Introduction   Conclusion   Implementation

Figure 9-2   Synthesize: Final Report (*continued*)

Two scenarios concern us— status quo and selective annexation

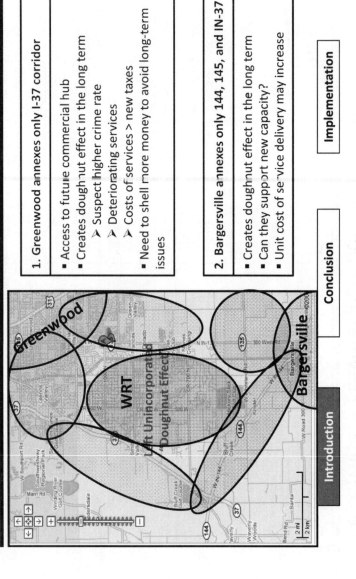

1. Greenwood annexes only I-37 corridor

   ■ Access to future commercial hub
   ■ Creates doughnut effect in the long term
      ▲ Suspect higher crime rate
      ▲ Deteriorating services
      ▲ Costs of services > new taxes
   ■ Need to shell more money to avoid long-term issues

2. Bargersville annexes only 144, 145, and IN-37

   ■ Creates doughnut effect in the long term
   ■ Can they support new capacity?
   ■ Unit cost of service delivery may increase

| Introduction | Conclusion | Implementation |

Figure 9-2 Synthesize: Final Report (*continued*)

The story at a glance

- **Introduction**
  - ▶ A team of Kelley faculty and students investigated incorporation options for Center Grove
  - ▶ The pro bono study spanned one year and included primary and secondary research
  - ▶ Center Grove is an upscale community with many strengths, but it faces several challenges due to dramatic growth—it should consider annexation or incorporation

- **Conclusion**
  - ▶ Incorporation could improve the safety and condition of roads
  - ▶ Incorporation could provide upgrades to important services such as police, waste, and water
  - ▶ Incorporation could allow more local control over zoning and lead to more green space and economic development

- **Implementation**
  - ▶ An incorporation would take several years but would have positive long-term impact
  - ▶ Incorporation could be financially feasible with funding through loans and bonds; it would require an increase in certain taxes
  - ▶ There are risks and challenges to completing the incorporation

Figure 9-2   Synthesize: Final Report (*continued*)

189

There are a significant number of unincorporated roads

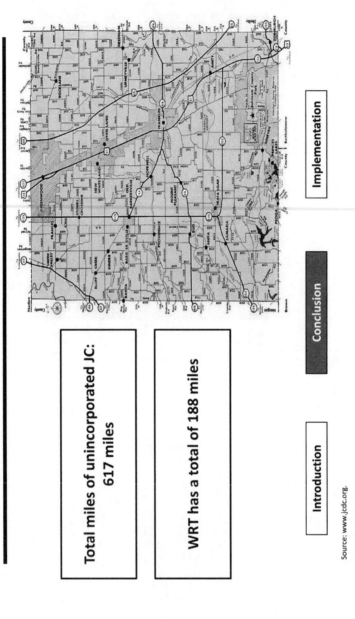

Total miles of unincorporated JC: 617 miles

WRT has a total of 188 miles

Introduction

Conclusion

Implementation

Figure 9-2 Synthesize: Final Report (*continued*)

Current condition of roads suggests room for improvement

"Police prohibited from chases on unincorporated roads"

"Citizens complain about potholes and excessive traffic"

Introduction

Conclusion

Implementation

Figure 9-2 Synthesize: Final Report (*continued*)

191

Safety is also a significant area of concern

Two collisions in less than one week

Many citizens have experienced near collisions at various crossings

INDOT Hazard Index Rating ranked Stones Crossing Road 1009 of more than 6000

Note: Citizens and county leaders are attempting to raise $1M to improve the situation

Introduction

Conclusion

Implementation

Source: 2007 Daily Journal Software.

Figure 9-2 Synthesize: Final Report (*continued*)

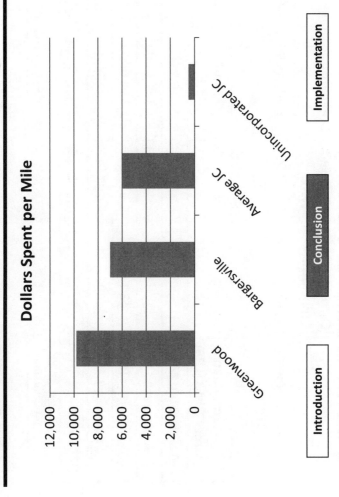

Figure 9-2   Synthesize: Final Report (*continued*)

Incorporation would increase funding for roads

	Current— Uninc. JC	Incorporated WRT	Greenwood	Bargersville
Motor Vehicle Highway Tax (MVH)	421,000	800,000	**1,409,000**	459,000
Local Road & Street Dist. (LRS)	0	600,000	**730,000**	328,000
Accelerated MVH	9,000	40,000	**70,000**	23,000
Accelerated LRS	0	120,000	**141,000**	65,000
Total	430,000	1,560,000	**2,350,000**	875,000
Funding / Mile	696/m	8,297/m*	**9,325/m**	8,454/m

*Note: This could be increased even further with special assessments not assumed here (e.g. wheel tax, etc.).

Introduction	Conclusion	Implementation

Source: Summary of Highway Revenues, Distributions and Expenses for Indiana Counties, Cities, and Towns—RP-4-2005.pdf.

Figure 9-2   Synthesize: Final Report (*continued*)

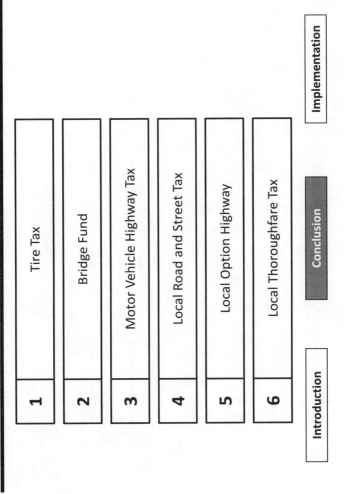

Incorporation of WRT will provide funding options

1	Tire Tax
2	Bridge Fund
3	Motor Vehicle Highway Tax
4	Local Road and Street Tax
5	Local Option Highway
6	Local Thoroughfare Tax

Introduction   Conclusion   Implementation

Source: Summary of Highway Revenues, Distributions and Expenses for Indiana Counties, Cities, and Towns–RP-4-2005.pdf.

Figure 9-2   Synthesize: Final Report (*continued*)

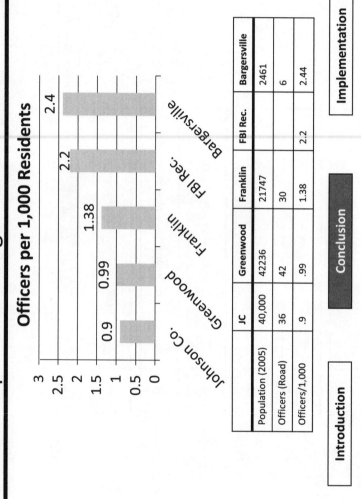

The current police coverage in WRT is low

Officers per 1,000 Residents

	JC	Greenwood	Franklin	FBI Rec.	Bargersville
Population (2005)	40,000	42236	21747		2461
Officers (Road)	36	42	30		6
Officers/1,000	.9	.99	1.38	2.2	2.44

Introduction   Conclusion   Implementation

Source: www.johnsoncountysheriff.com; www.city-data.com, http://www.jcdc.org; interviews; Stats Indiana.

Figure 9-2   Synthesize: Final Report (*continued*)

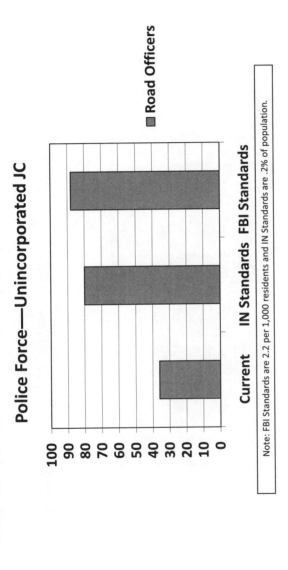

The recommended police force is significantly higher

Police Force—Unincorporated JC

■ **Road Officers**

Current   IN Standards   FBI Standards

Note: FBI Standards are 2.2 per 1,000 residents and IN Standards are .2% of population.

Introduction   Conclusion   Implementation

Source: Interviews; Stats Indiana; Indiana Law Enforcement Academy Standards (ILEA).

Figure 9-2   Synthesize: Final Report (*continued*)

Growth of water and waste services requires more capacity

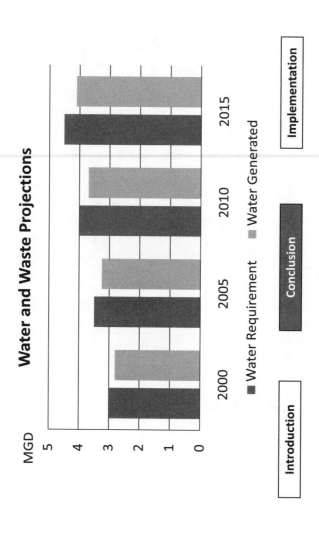

Figure 9-2   Synthesize: Final Report (*continued*)

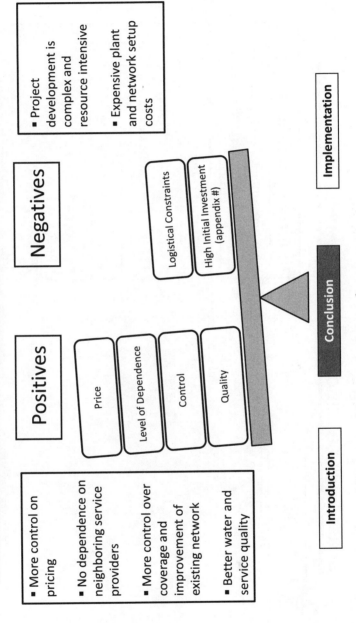

The pros of developing CG water and waste services outweigh the cons

Positives

- More control on pricing
- No dependence on neighboring service providers
- More control over coverage and improvement of existing network
- Better water and service quality

- Price
- Level of Dependence
- Control
- Quality

Negatives

- Logistical Constraints
- High Initial Investment (appendix #)

- Project development is complex and resource intensive
- Expensive plant and network setup costs

Introduction

Conclusion

Implementation

Figure 9-2 Synthesize: Final Report (*continued*)

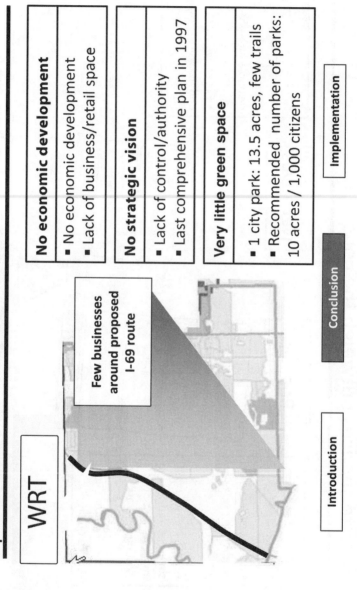

Figure 9-2　Synthesize: Final Report (*continued*)

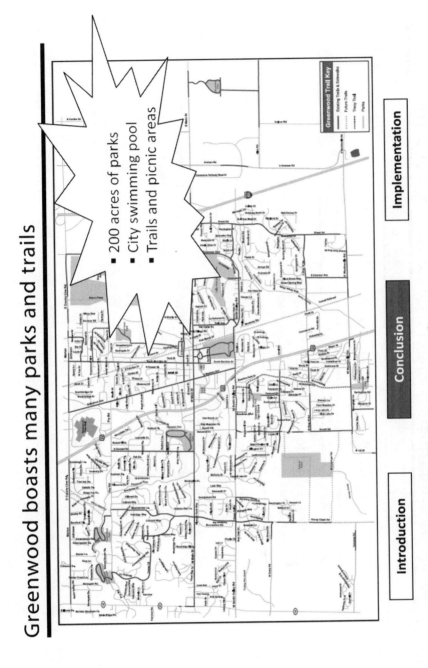

Figure 9-2 Synthesize: Final Report (*continued*)

201

The latest comprehensive plan expressed WRT concern

Johnson County Comprehensive Plan (1997)

- WRT predicted to become the most populous township in Johnson County
- Residents identified the following recreational concerns:

  ➢ Recreational land is a critical need in the township
  ➢ Pedestrian circulation issues need to be addressed and planned for future developments
  ➢ Require installation of sidewalks as opposed to street usage
  ➢ Maintain the current residential character of the township

| Introduction | Conclusion | Implementation |

Source: Comprehensive Plan Johnson County, IN; adopted April 1997.

Figure 9-2 Synthesize: Final Report (*continued*)

Ideas were discussed 10 years ago but not implemented

Creation of a park system specifically for White River Township

➤ A regional park within the White River floodplain
➤ Four non–site-specific community parks
➤ Three linear parks to directly link proposed parks, school complexes, and other destinations

| Introduction | Conclusion | Implementation |

Source: Comprehensive Plan Johnson County, IN; adopted April 1997.

Figure 9-2 Synthesize: Final Report (*continued*)

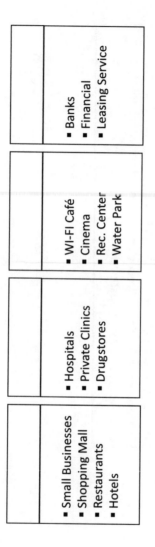

CG should seek to become a more complete community

Fully Functioning Community:

- Small Businesses
- Shopping Mall
- Restaurants
- Hotels

- Hospitals
- Private Clinics
- Drugstores

- WI-FI Café
- Cinema
- Rec. Center
- Water Park

- Banks
- Financial
- Leasing Service

Failure to act soon may result in limited land for such necessities in the future.

Introduction   Conclusion   Implementation

Figure 9-2   Synthesize: Final Report (*continued*)

The story at a glance

- **Introduction**
  - A team of Kelley faculty and students investigated incorporation options for Center Grove
  - The pro bono study spanned one year and included primary and secondary research
  - Center Grove is an upscale community with many strengths, but it faces several challenges due to dramatic growth——it should consider annexation or incorporation

- **Conclusion**
  - Incorporation could improve the safety and condition of roads
  - Incorporation could provide upgrades to important services such as police, waste, and water
  - Incorporation could allow more local control over zoning and lead to more green space and economic development

- **Implementation**
  - An incorporation would take several years but would have positive long-term impact
  - Incorporation could be financially feasible with funding through loans and bonds; it would require an increase in certain taxes
  - There are risks and challenges to completing the incorporation

Figure 9-2   Synthesize: Final Report (*continued*)

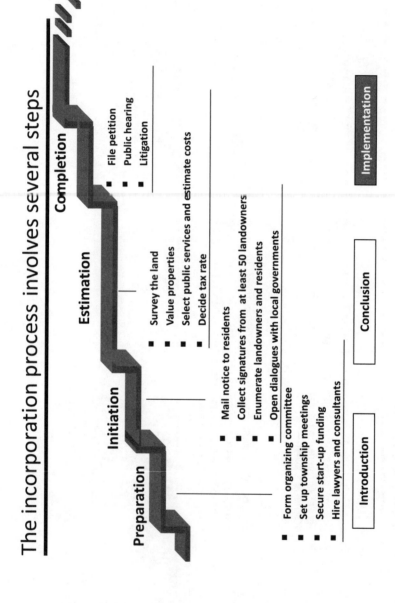

The incorporation process involves several steps

Preparation
- Form organizing committee
- Set up township meetings
- Secure start-up funding
- Hire lawyers and consultants

Initiation
- Mail notice to residents
- Collect signatures from at least 50 landowners
- Enumerate landowners and residents
- Open dialogues with local governments

Estimation
- Survey the land
- Value properties
- Select public services and estimate costs
- Decide tax rate

Completion
- File petition
- Public hearing
- Litigation

| Introduction | Initiation | Conclusion | Implementation |

Source: IC 36-5 Articles. Government of Towns (www.IN.gov).

Figure 9-2   Synthesize: Final Report (*continued*)

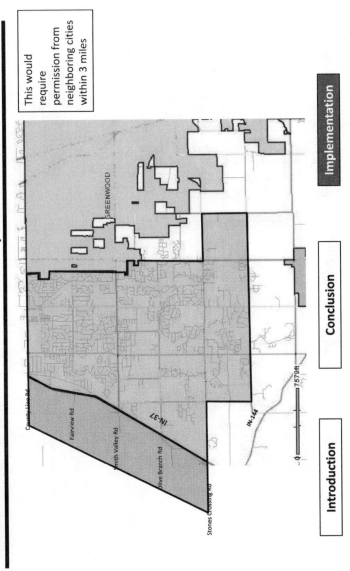

Figure 9-2 Synthesize: Final Report (*continued*)

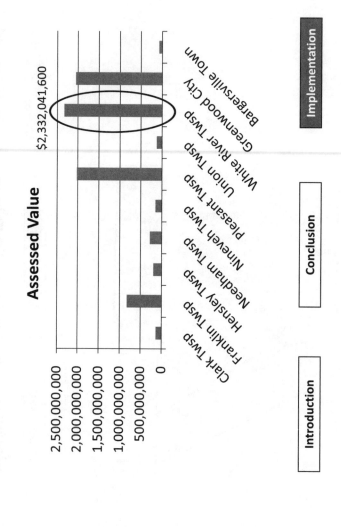

Figure 9-2 Synthesize: Final Report (*continued*)

But collects only a small amount of funding for services

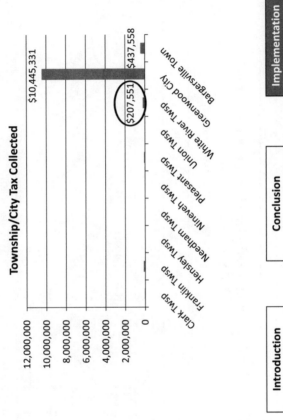

Figure 9-2   Synthesize: Final Report (*continued*)

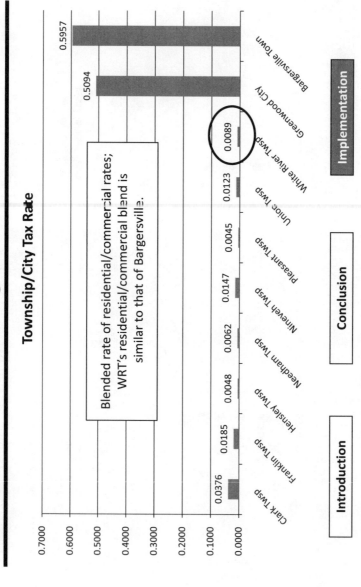

Source: Johnson County tax records.

Figure 9-2 Synthesize: Final Report (*continued*)

No city tax is collected or used in the CG area (only township)

White River Township——Unincorporated

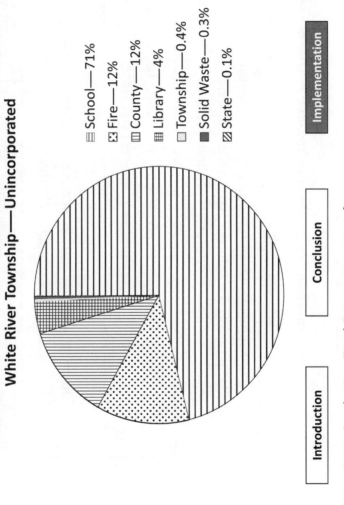

- ▤ School——71%
- ⠿ Fire——12%
- ▥ County——12%
- ▦ Library——4%
- ▨ Township——0.4%
- ■ Solid Waste——0.3%
- ▧ State——0.1%

| Introduction | Conclusion | Implementation |

Figure 9-2   Synthesize: Final Report (*continued*)

Municipal bonds are a way to raise money

Municipal bond rates are very low, in the 4.750% range

Municipal bond investors do not pay state or federal tax on the interest, so the yield can be lower than a corporation of similar risk

Bond insurance can increase the rating to AAA and further lower interest payment

In most states, a city can securitize bonds up to around 15% of aggregate assessed value

| Introduction | Conclusion | Implementation |

Figure 9-2 Synthesize: Final Report (*continued*)

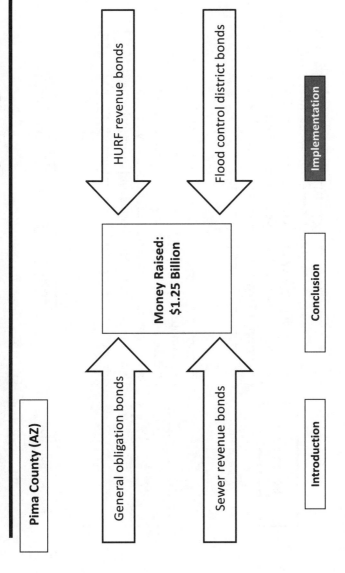

Figure 9-2 Synthesize: Final Report (*continued*)

Counties have successfully raised money through financing

Pima County (AZ)

HURF revenue bonds

Flood control district bonds

Money Raised: $1.25 Billion

General obligation bonds

Sewer revenue bonds

Introduction

Conclusion

Implementation

Source: Pima county bond election memo, October 2006.

We developed a model to test the financial feasibility

Revenues

- Modified tax structure to more closely resemble a city
- Personal property tax increases from 1.9 to 2.4%
- Conservatively did not model appreciation in values
- Conservatively did not model commercial taxes

Expenses

- Estimated $40 million to set up infrastructure
- Base estimates for ongoing city costs are $20M
- This estimate based on Greenwood city costs
- Interest expense from bonds and loans included

Introduction **Conclusion** **Implementation**

Figure 9-2   Synthesize: Final Report (*continued*)

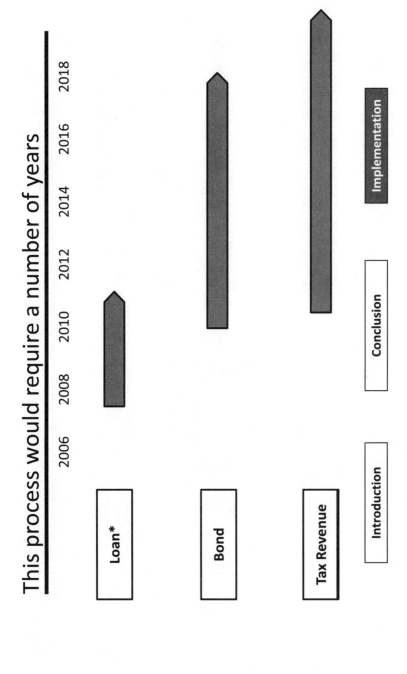

Figure 9-2 Synthesize: Final Report (*continued*)

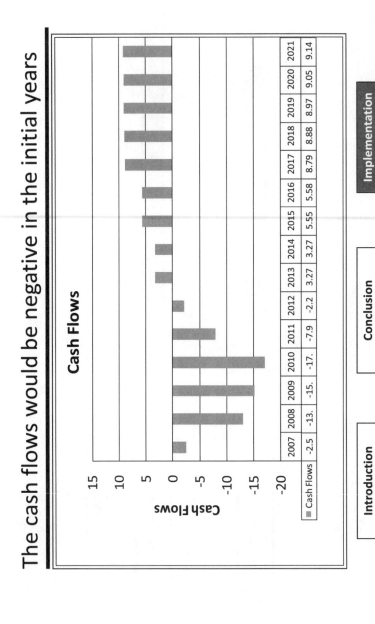

Source: Student analysis.

Figure 9-2 Synthesize: Final Report (*continued*)

216

Model assumptions

	Interest Rate
Bank Loan	5.50%
Bond	4.63%

	Year	$ Amount	
Loan	2007	2.55	mil $
Loan	2008	15.69	mil $
Loan Payment	2010	-18.25	mil $

	Year	$ Amount	
Bond Issue	2009	60.00	mil $
Bond Redeem	2021	-60.00	mil $

Introduction   Conclusion   Implementation

Figure 9-2 Synthesize: Final Report (*continued*)

The increases in property tax appear affordable

Sensitivity analysis of the average household's annual total property tax

- Average house assessed value: $100,000
- Total property tax rate increase from 1.98% to 2.48%
- Total property value increase: 0% to 50%

	1.98%	1.99%	2.08%	2.18%	2.28%	2.38%	2.48%
0%	$1,980	$1,990	$2,080	$2,180	$2,280	$2,380	$2,480
10%	$2,178	$2,189	$2,288	$2,398	$2,508	$2,618	$2,728
20%	$2,376	$2,388	$2,496	$2,616	$2,736	$2,856	$2,976
30%	$2,574	$2,587	$2,704	$2,834	$2,964	$3,094	$3,224
40%	$2,772	$2,786	$2,912	$3,052	$3,192	$3,332	$3,472
50%	$2,970	$2,985	$3,120	$3,270	$3,420	$3,570	$3,720

Introduction Conclusion Implementation

Figure 9-2   Synthesize: Final Report (*continued*)

There will be significant hurdles to overcome

Challenges	Solutions
Not enough support from local residents	Educate residents and gain their support
Insufficient start-up funding to cover the incorporation cost	Try to recruit volunteers and attract pro bono services
Difficult to persuade county officials to give up control	Communicate the benefits of incorporation to county officials
Possible remonstration from local residents	Ensure internal buy-in and prepare for potential litigation
Objection from nearby towns/cities	Open dialogues to ensure cooperation

Introduction   Conclusion   **Implementation**

Figure 9-2 Synthesize: Final Report (*continued*)

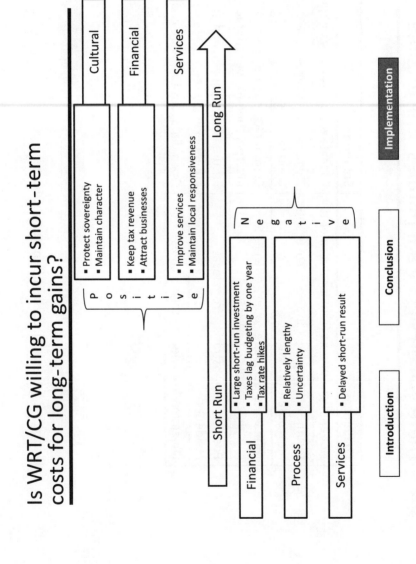

Figure 9-2 Synthesize: Final Report (*continued*)

The story at a glance

■ **Introduction**

ʌ A team of Kelley faculty and students investigated incorporation options for Center Grove

ʌ The pro bono study spanned one year and included primary and secondary research

ʌ Center Grove is an upscale community with many strengths, but it faces several challenges due to dramatic growth——it should consider annexation or incorporation

■ **Conclusion**

ʌ Incorporation could improve the safety and condition of roads

ʌ Incorporation could provide upgrades to important services such as police, waste, and water

ʌ Incorporation could allow more local control over zoning and lead to more green space and economic development

■ **Implementation**

ʌ An incorporation would take several years but would have positive long-term impact

ʌ Incorporation could be financially feasible with funding through loans and bonds; it would require an increase in certain taxes

ʌ There are risks and challenges to completing the incorporation

Figure 9-2 Synthesize: Final Report (*continued*)

221

AFTERWORD

I hope you have found some value in this book. I use the material with business school students, consultants, and executives on a regular basis, and it seems to resonate well with them. The goal was to present these concepts in a fairly straightforward and easy to grasp way. The key to making the framework lies not just in an understanding of the concepts, but also in disciplined execution of those concepts. The benefits of the model are best realized when the entire team is aware of and on board with the concepts; otherwise, the efficiency and effectiveness benefits may be somewhat lower. This brief and final chapter is dedicated to providing a few more ideas and examples of ways to implement the TEAM FOCUS model.

BUSINESS SCHOOL APPLICATIONS

One of the most obvious opportunities for application of the concepts in this book is within business schools. In my research in the area of management education (not to mention "hanging my hat" in business schools for the past 11 years), I enjoy tracking curriculum trends. One of the most significant shifts over the past 20 years has been a dramatic increase in "experiential learning" in the form of field studies, simulations, and case competitions. The ideas from this book may have something to offer in each of these areas.

For example, almost all top business schools provide opportunities for students to participate on consulting teams that work with actual businesses to solve real-world business problems. TEAM FOCUS could serve as a methodology for teams working on these projects. The deliverables provided in the book may offer ideas for templates that business consulting teams can consider as they work on these projects. The same can be said for business simulations and case competitions. As a coach for many such teams, I find that the students really appreciate any tools that can improve their efficiency—many competitions must result in a final slide deck and presentation in 24 hours! What great training to become a management consultant.

Another area of potential impact is in preparation for case interviews. As a consulting faculty member, one of my responsibilities is preparing students for case interviews. Consulting firms use case interviews to get a sense of the candidate's interpersonal and analytical ability. The TEAM component of the model can provide ideas on potential answers for behavioral questions as well as advice on how to act during the case interview. The FOCUS component is perfectly aligned with conducting the case interview with a very structured approach, as the intent of the interviewers is to simulate a "mini" project and see how well you can structure an answer and work toward recommendations in 30 to 40 minutes (this parallels actual consulting projects, just in a much-abbreviated format). One of my students mentioned that during an interview with a top consulting firm, she actually cited the framework and it seemed to help. She was asked how she would define good teamwork, and her answer included the inclusion of talking, evaluating, assisting, and motivating. Her interviewer was pleased, and the student ended up landing the summer internship at the firm.

Finally, some of this material could be considered as part of the core curriculum in management consulting and perhaps even the entire MBA program. *BusinessWeek*, *U.S. News & World Report*, and other periodicals (such as *Strategy & Business*) continue to highlight the need to advance students' skills in the areas of teamwork, analysis, and presentations ("TAP" skills) as well as the scientific method. Each of these topics is addressed to some extent in this book, with tools and templates being provided through the case study.

CONSULTING FIRM APPLICATIONS

Another obvious potential area of impact would be within consulting firms. My research suggests that most large consulting firms have developed their own internal problem-solving methodologies, which are probably quite similar to what is described in this book (at least for strategy and operations types of firms). Therefore, it may behoove new consultants to read this book as an introduction to and example of what they may experience in their new careers. Another opportunity for the large firms is to use this material in their introductory consulting courses as students are brought on board. An even more thorough indoctrination to the consulting mindset may be possible by reading all three books in the "McKinsey Trilogy"—*The McKinsey Way, The McKinsey Mind*, and *The McKinsey Engagement* (shameless plug for Ethan and me, I know).

For small- to medium-sized consulting firms, the opportunity for application may even be greater. I have had the privilege of working with two such consulting firms in Indianapolis over the past few years, and they seem to have been quite successful in integrating the concepts from the book into their core problem-solving methodologies.

The first is ABG, a consulting division of Adayana, which specializes in food, agriculture, and other related industries. Its consulting division was growing quickly and was focused on solving strategic, marketing, and operations issues for top companies in this space, such as John Deere, Monsanto, and others. I was brought in to teach a one-week course on the TEAM FOCUS model, and it went extremely well. The company ultimately adopted TEAM FOCUS as its internal framework, published a guidebook, and provided additional material and templates with many customized to their niche positioning.

The other firm is Walker Information, a well-established market research firm that is greatly expanding its value-adding consulting capabilities (it is very well known for its insights into customer loyalty). I was brought in to teach the TEAM FOCUS model and worked with the company as it took the ideas behind the TEAM FOCUS model and created its own custom methodology (SISTEM—Situation Analysis, Information and Fact Gathering, Strategy Development, Training, Execution, and Monitoring), which is now used on every engagement. The program had immediate impact during the second-year program, as members of the firm were teaching the ideas and implementing them on a case study and on real projects. The CEO, Steve Walker, told me that these ideas have "transformed the organization."

CORPORATE APPLICATIONS

These same concepts can be helpful to corporate executives as well. I present the model as a way to "think strategically," as it forces objective, scientific analysis. This is very important in this day and age, as intuition and executive blind spots can lead to significant loss of shareholder value in many cases. This model can become part of executive training on team problem solving and strategic thinking. The concepts presented herein can certainly be generalized to corporate team problem solving and even everyday work.

Another benefit to corporate executives is that the book can provide a window into the often-mysterious consulting approach to problem solving. This can prove invaluable if you are hiring or working with an external consulting firm. I have received numerous positive comments from both executives and consultants who thought that material from *The McKinsey Mind* actually led to a better company-consultant relationship, as the two groups were able to speak the same language and better understand the consulting problem-solving approach.

Finally, there has been a dramatic increase in internal consulting divisions within companies. This is partially due to a plethora of ex-consultants who left consulting to pursue a better lifestyle and who wanted to work within one company or one industry for a longer period of time. It is also a result of corporations realizing that there is value to having an independent perspective on decisions, even it comes from within the same corporation (internal consultants are usually separate from any one functional area). Internal consulting teams can utilize the ideas presented here on their projects as well as in training. Alumni from my classes have written me to let me know that they have utilized and even developed modules with this material for firms as large as 3M.

OUTCOMES OF THE CASE STUDY (FROM TIM'S PERSPECTIVE)

The story came together well in the end. During the dry run and final presentation, we received valuable feedback from the client and were able to respond to client concerns about our recommendations by discussing the factors that we had balanced and the outcomes that would result from different methods of incorporation. The impact of our presentation seemed most obvious when an older member of the community, a farmer, stood up to observe that the community had changed a great deal in the time he had lived there, from a quiet, dirt-road, rural community to a fast-growing area with high land values and new service needs. His point was not that change was bad, but rather that change was inevitable, and that the community needed to work toward positive change. The impact of our work hit home as I watched this farmer speak, and I realized that we were contributing to the future of a large number of individuals. I'm proud to have helped the community to understand its options so that it could forge ahead with an informed outlook and a united vision. Our principled approach helped to ensure that our contribution was a positive one.

At the end of the day, it was the community's responsibility to make a decision; the nature of the project was such that we simply put the information into people's hands and walked away. This differs from many consulting engagements, where a small initial project might lead to further work in the future. Another point I might make is that this project was so unusual (literally—new cities don't appear very often!) that it forced us to really test our methods and structure our thinking to a greater degree than a typical business case might have done. Despite the difficulties we had, I think it was a great learning experience, and I feel more confident about applying Dr. Friga's TEAM FOCUS model in the future, whatever the engagement might be.

Not only has the final report been read by many citizens, but the county leaders also refer to it as they shape their strategy going forward. The powers that be initially leaned toward annexation by Bargersville (ironically, our original hypothesis) instead of incorporation, which was our ultimate recommendation. However, they are now exploring the possibility of tidily merging with Barg-ersville, avoiding many of the headaches of annexation.

OUTCOMES OF THE CASE STUDY (FROM PAUL'S PERSPECTIVE)

Perhaps the impact of which I am most proud from writing this book is what happened to the subject of the case study presented in this book. The unincorporated area of White River Township has struggled for many, many years to make the strategic decisions nec-essary to advance the well-being of its citizens. It is a wonderful area in which to live, but it desperately needs changes in its infra-structure and organizational capabilities.

As a result of our project, hundreds of citizens are now engaged in the process of figuring out that strategy. There is a core team that took the ideas and ran with them; this team is currently crafting a strategy that will most likely lead to incorporation for White River Township. The ironic point is that it is looking as though that may come through a merger with Bargersville, which was our initial hypothesis! Ultimately, we felt that this hypothesis lacked sufficient support, as we assumed that the citizens would reject such a pro-posal. The current team of citizen and government leaders is work-ing hard to make it work. We certainly hope it will. I am extremely proud of our team and the potential impact on improving the long-term viability of the area and its 40,000 citizens!

Anita Knowles, the county council member who worked closely with our team, summarized our impact as shown here. It was an absolute pleasure working with her!

The case study has proven very beneficial to our commu-nity. There are three reasons why: this is the first time an objective, all-inclusive study of the area has been conducted; interesting conclusions were offered; and our community is now taking steps to accomplish one of the recommendations of the final report. I was amazed at how much the team accomplished in such a short period of time. I can safely say that this was both as efficient and effective a project as I have seen in quite some time.

The TEAM FOCUS Rules of Engagement

TEAM

Talk
- Communicate constantly
- Listen attentively
- Separate issues from people

Evaluate
- Discuss group dynamics
- Set expectations and monitor results
- Develop and reevaluate a personal plan

Assist
- Leverage expertise
- Keep teammates accountable
- Provide timely feedback

Motivate
- Identify unique motivators
- Positively reinforce teammates
- Celebrate achievements

FOCUS

Frame
- Identify the key question
- Develop the issue tree
- Formulate hypotheses

Organize
- Develop a high-level process map
- Create a content map to test hypotheses
- Design the story line

Collect
- Design "ghost charts" to exhibit necessary data
- Conduct meaningful interviews
- Gather relevant secondary data

Understand
- Identify the "so what(s)"
- Think through the implications for all constituents
- Document the key insight on all charts

Synthesize
- Obtain input and ensure buy-in from client
- Offer specific recommendations for improvement
- Tell a good story

1

231

INDEX OF STORIES FROM THE FIELD

FRAME

ORGANIZE

COLLECT

LIST OF ILLUSTRATIONS

FRAME

ORGANIZE

COLLECT

UNDERSTAND

SYNTHESIZE

INDEX

ABOUT THE AUTHOR

Dr. Paul N. Friga is an associate professor at the Kenan-Flagler School of Business at the University of North Carolina at Chapel Hill, where he teaches courses in management consulting and strategy. He also serves as the director of the consulting concentrations for undergraduates and MBAs. He researches strategic decision-making, knowledge transfer, intuition, management consulting processes, and entrepreneurship, and has presented at numerous conferences throughout the world. He is the recipient of several teaching awards and was appointed to the Strategic Management Society task force on teaching strategy. He completed his Ph.D. and MBA at the University of North Carolina at Chapel Hill and previously worked as a management consultant for Pricewaterhouse-Coopers and McKinsey & Company. Dr. Friga's undergraduate degree is from Saint Francis University, with a double degree in management and accounting. He has also earned CPA and CMA designations. Dr. Friga has consulted for numerous large (Fortune 100), mid-size, and entrepreneurial companies, as well as for universities and not-for-profit organizations. He is active in his community and church and resides in Chapel Hill, North Carolina, with his wife, Meredith, and son, Nicholas. He welcomes readers to view many of his ideas, papers, and slide decks at his Web site www.paulfriga.com.